Dedications

Bruce Lee

Sifu Wang

Warnings and Disclaimers

The information in this series of publications (Survival Fitness Plan Self-Defense Series) is made public for reference only.

Neither the author, publisher, nor anyone else involved in the production of this series is responsible for how the reader uses the information or the result of his/her actions.

Consult a physician before undertaking any new form of physical activity.

Contents

Introduction

It is my belief that Bruce Lee intended Jeet Kune Do to be a framework to be built upon in order for an individual to develop a way of fighting that works best for him/her -self.

Inside this book are lessons which focus on the base concepts and techniques that Bruce Lee developed for Jeet Kune Do. This could be interpreted as Bruce Lee's Jeet Kune Do, but what works for Bruce may not work for you, and what works for you may not work for me.

Use the lessons in this book as a base for you to create your own Jeet Kune Do. Once you understand them you will be well equipped to analyze any technique from any other source and decide if it will be useful to you, and if it is not, then get rid of it. That includes techniques in this book that you feel don't benefit you.

Learning many techniques is not what is needed to be a good fighter. It is far better to be very good at just a few than just okay at many. The key is to shed that which is not good for you. The more techniques you have in your "arsenal" for a certain situation means you have more things to choose from. It takes time to make choices, and the more you have to choose from, the longer it takes. It is far better to have one technique per situation that you know works, and then drill that into your muscle memory so if/when that situation comes up you will move instinctively. When you have these techniques instilled into your muscle memory you will not have to think about reacting in certain situations and your mind will be free to strategize.

In order to find the best technique for you to use in a situation experimentation is needed. That is what training is for. When choosing, keep to the main JKD principles/concepts.

This book focuses on the physical techniques and mental strategies of fighting and does attempt to explore the philosophical or spiritual side of JKD. **Bruce Lee's the Tao of Jeet Kune Do** is (in my opinion) the best source for anyone interested in that side of JKD and is highly recommended even for those who are not.

Sam Fury

Jeet Kune Do Concepts

Before starting the lessons in this book it is recommended to read this chapter so you can get a feel for the main concepts of Jeet Kune Do. Some of these concepts are also discussed in greater detail as part of the lessons. Like everything in this book, treat these things as guidelines to be adhered to *most* of the time, not strict rules set in stone.

Lead Straight Punch

"The leading straight punch is the backbone of all punching in Jeet Kune Do."

Bruce Lee.

The lead straight punch is designed to be fast, accurate, powerful and extremely practical. A lesson is dedicated to the lead straight punch.

Non-Telegraphed Attacks

Telegraphing an attack is when you do something that alerts your opponent to your attack such as pulling your hand back before punching, looking at your intended target, or even just a slight twitch in your face.

When you can initiate your attack without any forewarning your opponent will have less time to react.

Jeet Kune Do attacks are meant to be thrown with no signs of preparation, but even this is not set-in-stone. An example may be when you have your opponent's arms pinned. Pulling your arm back will produce more power and because you have his/her arms pinned telegraphing may not matter.

Non-Classical

Every situation is different and to be successful you must be able to adapt. Being set in a particular style of martial arts and their classical forms can restrict the practitioner.

"Empty your mind, be formless, shapeless, like water. If you put water into a cup, it becomes the cup. You put water into a bottle and it becomes the bottle. You put it in a teapot it becomes the teapot. That water can flow, or it can crash. Be water, my friend."

Bruce Lee.

Furthermore, many of the traditional forms are designed to look good as opposed to actually being effective. In JKD effectiveness is what matters.

Economy of Motion

Economy of motion is minimizing waste of time and/or movement. A good attack will reach its target in the least amount of time with as much force as possible. This saves you energy and also makes your attack faster giving your opponent less time to react.

Directness
Your attack should take the shortest possible route to its target while you stay safe from your opponent's attack. This is usually a straight line.

Your Longest Weapon to the Closest Target
By using your lead hand or foot to the closest target results in your attack traveling the shortest distance possible, which means your opponent has less time to react. An example of this is the low lead side kick to the shin or knee.

Simplicity
Do not complicate things. Only do as much as is needed to achieve your objective as quickly as possible.

"Simplicity is the shortest distance between two points."

Bruce Lee

Simultaneous Defense and Offence
In many of the fighting arts when an attack comes in the practitioner defends and then returns with an attack of his/her own (a counter-attack). It is one after the other. With simultaneous defense and offence, when the attack comes in you defend and counter at the same time. This saves time and is harder for your opponent to defend against.

A counter-attack is a tactic employed in response to your opponent's attack, also referred in this book as a counter, countering etc.

Interception
Interception goes one step further on simultaneous defense and offence by making the defense and offense one movement. You stop your opponent's attack with an attack of your own. In other words, you intercept his/her attack.

The two main tools for doing this are the stop hit and sliding leverage which are explained in detail in their respective dedicated lessons.

Jeet Kune Do literally translates to "The Way of the Intercepting Fist".

Four Ranges of Combat

There are four basic ranges that you can be in relation to your opponent and the attacks that can be made. You must know how to effectively fight in all of them. The ranges are kicking, punching, trapping and grappling.

Five Ways of Attack

Although presented separately, the five ways of attack work together and are very much intertwined. What follows is a very basic overview. Each way of attack will be discussed in detail in the lessons.

Single Angulated Attack (SAA)

A single attack directed at the target using the most economical route possible. It is hitting your opponent before he/she can effectively respond. It relies on speed and timing.

Attack by Combination (ABC)

An attack which is made up of two or more movements which, preferably, blend together in a natural manner.

Immobilization Attack (IA)

Trapping or immobilizing your opponent's limb(s) so you can either direct it/them out of your attack line and/or immobilize it/them.

Progressive Indirect Attack (PIA)

Using a feint or other movement to create an opening and then striking in the same movement, i.e., you do not withdraw your limb to make the strike.

Attack by Drawing (ABD)

Exposing a target in order to entice your opponent to attack. When he/she is committed to an attack you intercept or defend and counter.

Centerline

The following is an excerpt from **Basic Wing Chun by Sam Fury** (available at **SurviveTravel.com/Wing-Chun**).

---Start of Excerpt---

The center-line principle is a core concept in Wing Chun Kung Fu. Most, if not all of the exercises in this book are focused on protecting your own center-line while controlling your opponent's. Controlling the position of your center-line in relation to your opponent's is done with footwork. Understanding the center-line will allow you to instinctively know where your opponent is.

Your centerline is an imaginary line drawn vertically down the center of your body. All the vital organs are located near the center of the body. Keep it away from your opponent by angling it away from him/her.

Your central-line (different from your center-line) is drawn from your angled center to your opponent.

Offensively, you generate the most power when punching out from your center since you can incorporate your whole body and hips.

When attacking in a straight line your center-line is away from your opponent while your central-line faces his/her center.

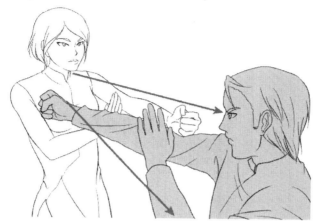

With hook punches and other circular attacks, the center- and central-lines merge.

There are three main guidelines for the centerline.

- The one who controls the centerline will control the fight.
- Protect and maintain your own centerline while you control and exploit your opponent's.
- Control the centerline by occupying it.

-----End of Excerpt-----

How to Use This Book to Train in Jeet Kune Do

How often and how long your training sessions are depend on the time you have available and the time you are willing to spend. Like everything, the more you train, the faster you will progress.

Warm up

Always begin your training session with a warm up and light stretching. Not warming up before putting the body through strenuous activity will result in injury.

The length of time you spend warming up depends on your body and the temperature. The cooler the temperature, the more time you will need to warm up.

Skipping Rope

Skipping rope for three to five minutes is usually sufficient to warm up. Skipping will also help develop a sense of balance and the ability to be "light on your feet".

Longer skipping sessions can be used to increase cardiovascular stamina. Ten minutes of skipping rope has the same cardiovascular benefits as thirty minutes of jogging.

To get the most out of skipping add some variety such as holding one foot out in front of you while skipping on the other, alternating the feet with each turn of the rope, varying the speed of which you skip, etc. Use your wrists to swing the rope as opposed to your arm.

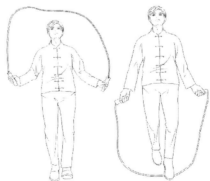

A leather rope with ball bearings in the handles is the best kind of skipping rope to use.

Shadow Boxing

Shadow boxing is another good warm-up activity which helps build stamina, speed, muscle memory, footwork, creation of ideas, etc. When you do it imagine an opponent in front of you and get yourself into a fighting frame of mind. Start slow and relaxed concentrating on form. Build up speed as your body warms up.

Focused Activities

Skipping rope and shadow boxing are good for warming up the body as a whole but you must also pay special attention to the actions you plan to do during the training session and imitate them during the warm up. For example, if you will be practicing the side kick then do some light kicking before attempting to do them with more power.

Stretching

Light stretching is also needed as part of your warm-up. Deep stretching is done after your workout.

Skills

Work on technical skills immediately after your warm up. Technical skills are best done while you are fresh. If you do them when fatigued you will probably not do them properly and how you train will reflect in the way you fight. When you start getting exhausted switch to more endurance based training.

Progressive Learning

Each chapter in this book can be considered a lesson and the way this book is presented gives these lessons in a progressive manner. It is advised that you do not skip lessons/chapters, at least for the first time you go through them. Repeating lessons is encouraged, including during the first time you go through them.

Each lesson focuses on one skill or stratagem. It is intended that the focus of your training session will be on that lesson but you should incorporate and adapt what you have previously learned where appropriate, including various training exercises.

Everything in fighting is intertwined and works together!

Practice everything on both sides of your body i.e. from a right and left lead stance.

Spend as much time as you need on each lesson. Sometimes you may which to spend a whole training session on one lesson and others you can do multiple lessons.

When learning something new it is important that you first do it slowly to get the correct technique. After you have the technique you can work on other things such as speed, power, using the technique with other movements, etc. Revisit perfecting technique regularly.

Here are some different methods in which you can practice a new movement once you have a good grasp of correct technique. They are by no means the only ways. Training methods are only limited to imagination.

> Increase speed and power in the air whilst standing still.

> Use the technique with footwork and/or *evasive movements.

> Practice the technique by striking something, e.g., paper, punching bag, punching pads.

> Practice striking a moving target such as a partner moving a hand pad or a light ball hanging from the ceiling.

> Practice doing a movement on the instruction of a stimulus e.g. when someone claps you do the movement.

> Have a partner reveal a punching pad as he/she moves around (good for training your perception and response.)

> Do the movement with parries, as a counter, in combination etc.

> Incorporate the movement in shadow boxing.

> One person attacks while the other defends.

> Practice the movement/strategy while sparring.

In the spirit of Jeet Kune Do, find what works best for you and discard what doesn't. Use your training to experiment with what you learn. When you discover things that work well, train in them more often, for these are the things you will want to use in a real fight.

*An evasive movement is using your body to move away from an attack, i.e., there is no contact (as opposed to blocking or parrying). Ideally, your evasive maneuver will cause the attack to miss you by as little as possible and keep you in distance to counter-attack.

Sparring

Sparring is the closest thing you can do to actually fighting and it is introduced as a lesson as soon as some of the basics have been covered. Once you have done the lesson on sparring make it a regular occurrence. Use sparring to test what you learn on a reactive opponent. Having some sparring time in every training session is recommended, and you may even want to have whole sessions with just sparring.

Fitness

Jeet Kune Do stresses the importance of personal health and fitness more than many other martial arts. Having separate training sessions dedicated to increasing fitness is recommended. The cross training will also allow you to learn different skills and prevents training slumps which can occur.

Skipping has already been mentioned as a good fitness activity. Even just 3 three minute rounds of skipping with 30 to 60 second breaks in-between can make for a good workout.

Intense sparring is also good for fitness.

Things like running, cycling, rock climbing, parkour, swimming etc. are good for fitness and you will be learning/practicing skills that may prove very useful. **Survival Fitness by Sam Fury** (available at **SurviveTravel.com/Survival-Fitness**) is a good source of information for training in these activities.

Most team-sports are also great for fitness, especially those requiring short bursts of running such as soccer (football), basketball etc.

Muscle conditioning must also be worked on. It can be done with only bodyweight exercises, or you may prefer to use weights. If working with weights remember that heavy weights will build mass (bulking-up), where-as lighter weights will build density (carving the muscles or "getting ripped").

To increase endurance you need to train until exhaustion. Use fartlek style training where you intersperse moderate-intensity exercise with high-intensity bursts. For example, if you go for a 30 minute jog then every two minutes put in a ten second sprint.

Stretch/Cool down

End every training session with a cool down. A cool down is a light version of a warm-up followed by a deeper stretching. How long your cool down is up to you. It should be at least as long as it takes for your heart rate to return to normal.

Training for Reality

It is important that you train the way you will fight because what you do in training will be instilled in your body. If you punch incorrectly and/or with no effort during training, then essentially you are teaching your body how to punch in a less effective or incorrect way.

Everything you do should be with 100% concentrated effort.

When hitting a pad or in the air imagine an opponent and where you are aiming.

If you want to become fast you have to train with fast movements. This does not mean you over-exert and tense up, for that is awkward and brings with it bad technique. You must be relaxed with smooth movements.

If learning for self-protection, train most in that which is most effective. During sparing you can figure out what techniques work most often for you.

Indoors Vs Outdoors

When you need to use certain equipment or need a controlled environment to practice technical skills and the weather is bad it is better to train indoors. For everything else, train outside, regardless of the weather. In a real fight it may be hot, cold, very bright, foggy, raining, etc. Only by actually training in these circumstances can you get used to them.

On Guard Position

The On-Guard Position (OGP) is an effective fighting stance which allows you to be balanced during movement. It is a perfect stance to attack and defend without telegraphing.

Wide stances found in many traditional martial arts are good for stability but lack in mobility and often leave target areas open. A narrow stance such as in boxing is good for mobility but lacks in stability and leaves the groin and other low target areas open. The On-Guard Position is both stable and mobile and is designed to protect all major target areas.

Lead and Rear Sides

Your lead side (leg, foot, arm, hand) is whichever side you put forward most. Your rear side is which-ever side is not your lead.

When adopting the OGP your dominant side is your lead most of the time. Since your lead arm and leg are closest to your opponent you will use them for the majority of your strikes. Having your dominant side as your lead means that the majority of your strikes will be faster and stronger (as opposed to having your weak side as your lead).

Striking with your lead will never be as powerful as striking with your rear because there is less momentum, but the speed advantage gained is worth the tradeoff. In training work hard on improving power from your lead arm and leg.

Although your lead is mainly for striking and your rear is mainly for defense there are no hard rules and you will often need to defend and attack with either hand.

In attack, your lead is best used for speed and your rear for power.

Whichever hand is attacking, the other is returning to protect the body or doing some other defensive maneuver, such as pinning your opponent's arm. The defensive hand also needs to be ready to perform a follow-up strike.

Although your dominant side is your main lead and is how you should fight in real situations, in training train on both sides, taking turns between left and right leads. This will ensure body balance and will also prepare you in case you are unable to use your dominant side as your lead, e.g., due to injury.

These pictures are from a right lead.

Matched and Un-Matched Leads

When both you and your opponent have the same lead, e.g., both in a right lead, it is referred to as a matched lead. If you have different leads it is called an un-matched lead.

If you are against an opponent with an unmatched lead place your lead foot slightly to the outside of your opponent's lead foot. This puts you outside his/her guard which gives you more time to react to his/her movements. It also keeps you away from your opponent's rear arm and leg.

Lower Body

The OGP is a semi-crouched position.

Stand naturally with your feet shoulder width apart then take a natural step forward with your dominant foot. If needed, adjust your feet so that they are a little wider than shoulder width apart. Keep your knees slightly bent.

Your knees and elbows are never be locked straight when fighting.

Keep your lead knee fairly straight and turn it slightly inward to protect your groin. In order to stay light on your feet your lead heel has only light ground contact.

Your torso forms a straight line with your lead leg. The position of your lead foot will determine the structure of your torso. What you do depends on your intention. If your lead foot is turned inward it will give you a narrower profile which is good for defense. Some attacks will require a wider profile so you will need to turn your foot outward. In a neutral stance, have your lead foot at a 25° to 30° angle.

Place your rear foot at a 45° to 50° angle with your heel raised.

The raised heel enhances mobility. It will allow for a quick shifting of weight when advancing as well as some give when defending.

Your feet are directly under your body. When in a neutral position (neither attacking nor defending) your weight is spread evenly over both legs, or slightly more over your lead foot.

To put more weight on your lead just bend your lead knee a little more.

Upper Body

Hold your lead shoulder slightly raised with your chin slightly lowered to protect it. Your chin and lead shoulder meet about half-way.

Both your hands help to protect your face and groin. Your lead hand hovers just below shoulder height. Your rear hand is at approximately chest height and about five inches away from your body.

Hold your elbows close to your body to protect your torso. They must remain relaxed but sturdy, i.e., they can move side to side if needed but should withstand an attack without collapsing toward your body.

Your head is mobile to avoid getting hit. When fighting in-close the side of your chin can be tucked to your shoulder for more protection. In extreme defense, tuck the point of your chin to your shoulder.

Keep your back relaxed and partially contract your stomach muscles.

The OGP is a non-rigid stance. Be relaxed in position with your hands and body in constant light motion whilst keeping covered. Curved motions are more energy efficient than straight lines (such as if you have to change direction suddenly), but do not overdo it, and do not unnecessarily shift your weight from one foot to the other.

You may need to learn to keep your body relaxed. Do this with conscious effort until you can gain the feeling at will. You will then be able to induce this attitude in tense environments.

The above described is how to adopt the OGP in general, however, everything is dependent on the situation you are faced with.

Check you OGP in the mirror ensuring you are relaxed with no openings.

When practicing different techniques launch them from the OGP and return to the OGP as soon as possible.

When investigating the use of techniques from other sources, use those that are conducive to the OGP.

Balance

Balance is extremely important in fighting, both physically and in attitude. Without the ability to maintain balance you will be unable to attack or defend effectively.

Physical Balance

Physical balance must be attained whilst in motion. Having balance while being stationary is fine, but a fighter must not be stationary.

Balance is maintained by controlling your center of gravity, which is constantly changing depending on your movements. Correct body positioning, such as the OGP, and proper footwork will ensure this.

Keep your feet directly under your body and do not cross your feet.

You can tune into your body when in states of balance and relaxation. Place your body in balanced and non-balanced positions and consciously notice how your body feels. Move forward, back and from side to side.

Find opportunities to improve your balance during everyday life, e.g., stand on one foot while putting on your shoes.

Balance in Attitude

Balance in attitude is keeping an emotional evenness.

Acting in extreme emotional states, such as anger, will only hinder your ability. Having and showing intensity while fighting is a good thing, but acting without thinking, unless you have trained your body to do so (such as blocking a strike), is not. The energy must be channeled correctly.

Hold yourself in a confident humbleness.

Confidence will give you the winning attitude, but under-estimating any opponent is not wise. Treat every opponent as if they are well-trained, from the first strike to the last.

Learn to calm yourself in times of stress.

Footwork and Distance

Distance

The control of distance is very important in fighting. It is a constant effort to get the distance that is best for you. You want to make your opponent misjudge distance so you can land your strikes while evading his/hers.

Fighting Measure

The fighting measure is the distance you keep from your opponent. Ideally, you want it so you cannot be hit unless your opponent lunges at you. This gives you time to react to his/her actions. At the same time, you do not want to be too far away that you cannot attack.

You want to be just out of reach, so if he/she throws a simple punch it won't reach you, but you will be able to reach him/her with a small step forward.

The exact fighting measure is different for each person, and changes depending on your opponent. You have to allow for reach, speed, reaction time etc. of you in relation to your opponent. You also must consider the target areas your opponent is aiming for most.

Footwork

Distance is controlled mainly with footwork. Footwork allows you to evade an opponent's attacks while increasing power and speed in your own. All techniques require a foundation of good footwork to be effective.

Keep your steps springy, smooth (don't hop or drag your feet) and small, even when covering large distances. Use the balls of your feet to glide over the floor.

Two medium steps are better than one big one. This will help you keep balance and will also allow you to halt and/or change direction quickly. As with everything in JKD, there are exceptions to the rule and what you do depends on the situation.

When training, experiment using all techniques with all types of footwork. Advance, retreat, circle etc., before, while and after each technique. Test what works best for you and then train in those things regularly.

Shuffle on the balls of your feet between each maneuver. This is not dancing on your toes like a boxer showing off. That will only tire you out. Rather, it is simulating the fact that in a real fight you will have to keep moving to avoid being struck. Being in constant motion also allows you to move faster when needed.

Staying in one spot for too long is dangerous. Continuously change the distance using a variety of length, speed and angles in your steps. This will also help to confuse your opponent so he/she misjudges his/her own distance.

Variety is important in all aspects of fighting. You do not want to set a pattern that your opponent can capitalize on.

Shuffle

The shuffle is used to quickly move forward (advance) or back (retreat) to either employ an attack or avoid one.

Advance Shuffle

From the On-Guard Position move your front foot forward about half a step. Your rear foot then slides up to take your front foot's original position. Repeat this motion to advance further.

Throughout the movement ensure your guard is kept up and you knees are slightly bent and relaxed. Glide on the balls of your feet with your weight spread as evenly as you can over your legs. When advancing your lead foot your weight will favor that foot, but only for a very short time.

Retreat Shuffle

The retreat shuffle is the opposite of the advance shuffle. Your rear foot goes back about half a step and your front foot takes your rear foots original position.

As you slide your front foot back your weight will momentarily shift to your stationary rear foot. Keep your rear heel raised. Repeat this motion to retreat further.

Like all techniques, when practicing the shuffles, go slow to begin with until you are confident that you are retaining perfect balance. Add speed when ready. Practice on both sides, i.e., left and right leads.

When confident with single steps, do doubles and triples.

Shuffle on a Stimulus

A noise stimulus can be used to induce a reaction, e.g., a clap. You need someone to make the noise.

One clap (or whatever) is one movement, either forward or back. The forward and back movements alternate. Two claps means do two movements i.e. one forward and then one back.

This exercise can also be applied to double movements or whatever your imagination comes up with, e.g., strikes.

Lead Straight Punch

The lead straight punch is a fundamental technique of JKD and many very important lessons stem from it. It has been designed to be fast, accurate, powerful and extremely practical.

Eventually you want to be able to throw the straight punch (lead or rear) from any position that your hand happens to be in at any given time and without telegraphing your intention.

Forming a Fist

Knowing how to form a proper fist is essential in order to punch without injuring yourself.

Hold your hand out flat with your fingers together and your thumb up.

Roll your fingers into your palm and then bring your thumb down over your fingers.

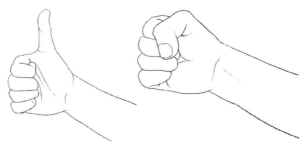

Conditioning your knuckles will make your punches stronger and help to prevent injury in the future. Doing push-ups on clenched fists is a good way to start. Do them with the knuckles from your two small fingers making contact with the floor, your palms facing each-other. This exercise has the added benefits of conditioning your muscles and ensures your wrists are in proper alignment with your forearms.

Delivery of the Lead Straight Punch

Stand relaxed in the OGP. During the delivery of the punch keep your rear hand up ready for defense and/or counter-attack.

Use your whole body to generate power.

The power comes up from the ground and through your hips with a twist on the ball of your foot. Whip your hand straight out in front of your nose from the center of your body.

To prevent telegraphing start your hand moving first.

Ideally, the point of contact for the lead straight is in line with the surface of your shoulder. If your target is lower or higher than this height then adjust the height of your shoulder-line to match, i.e., crouch or stand on the balls of your feet.

Your elbow stays in and close to your body. This helps with protection and also minimizes telegraphing.

As with all hand strikes, your weight slightly shifts over your front leg. This increases power and speed.

As your strike makes contact snap your wrist and clench your hand into a vertical fist with your thumb up and knuckles pointed toward your target. Your fist must be aligned with your forearm and not bent down at the wrist.

As you snap your lead your rear hand is drawn suddenly towards your body. The bottom three knuckles make contact as you punch through your target.

With all strikes, it is important that they end with a snap a few inches behind your target. You are striking through your opponent with a snap as opposed to pushing.

The pivot of your hips, the snap back of your rear hand and other body movements help to increase power in the lead straight, but these things will add to telegraphing your punch. Against a fast opponent you may have to sacrifice some power to increase the speed of the punch.

Allow your arm to come back naturally to the OGP. This will probably be in an elliptical shape but may be straight back depending on your posture. The important thing is that it does not drop down and leave an opening.

The whole punch is a continuous motion.

Keep your body upright and balanced throughout the movement. Leaning back will negate power. If you do lean back while fighting, e.g., to avoid getting hit, ensure you reposition your body before punching.

Leaning too far forward will cause you to become un-balanced. You must be committed to your strike but do not over-reach so that your balance is compromised. This over-reaching is usually a result of being too far away from your target. Use your footwork to close the distance, not the lean of your body. This applies to all strikes.

Trying to put too much body-weight behind the punch will also negate power. It will turn the punch into a push which may move your opponent back but will not have anywhere near the same devastating impact as a whip-like punch.

Never initiate a strike with a foot off the ground.

In relation to reach, the lead straight can be used short or long. The extension in reach is made by extending your shoulder into the strike. Use your whole reach whenever possible.

Developing Relaxation

Being relaxed is very important in producing speed and power. A simple exercise to develop a relaxed arm is to get someone to hold your arm in position. Give him/her the full weight of your arm. Gradually increase the tension until you have just enough to hold your arm up. Notice how relaxed your arm is. This is how relaxed it should be before initiating a strike.

Concurring and Overlapping Circles

As you strike the power comes in the form of a series of circular motions. In order to use your whole body to generate power you just need to imagine a centripetal force (a force that makes a body follow a curved path) flowing through your body from the ground up.

Your first movement starts with the turning of your rear ankle. This sets the body in motion.

The next circle is at the lead knee, followed by the waist, then the lead shoulder, then the lead arm and finally the lead wrist.

All these circles happen almost instantaneously and with increasing speed from one to the other. Your punch reaches its destination before the first circle stops and the last motion of your wrist is the fastest.

Using Your Hips

Learning to use your hips properly will help you develop power in your strikes.

Hang an A4 sized piece of paper from the ceiling so it is about chest height. Stand about eight inches away with both your feet parallel to it. Have your hands in front of your chest and let your elbows hang relaxed. Keep your eyes on the target whilst you twist on the balls of your feet in a clockwise direction. End at a 90° angle to the paper, facing your right. As you turn shift your body weight to your left leg.

Now you will turn anti-clockwise so you end up facing your left. This time initiate your hips in a sudden clockwise rotating motion as you pivot. Your shoulders automatically rotate after your hips and your weight will shift over each leg as needed. It is important that your shoulders follow your hips and not the other way round. It is your hips that provide momentum for the turn.

Next, as your body rotates raise your elbow to strike the target. Do this from left to right. When you are comfortable with the motion replace your elbow with your fists.

When you are ready, practice this from a left lead stance. Twist your body clockwise so that your shoulders are in-line with the target and with your weight mostly on your rear foot. Initiate an anti-clockwise movement with your hips and pivot on bath balls of your feet. Your rear heel rises and your weight shifts forward as you deliver a punch with your right hand. Your body ends facing the target.

Finally, practice this hip movement from a right lead OGP to deliver a lead straight punch. Advance from paper to harder targets such as a punching bag.

Producing the "Snap"

You can develop speed, power and the snap in your punches by holding a cylindrical weight in your hand as you punch. When you are relaxed the weight will cause the punch to automatically snap back.

When you do not have the weights just imagine that you are still holding them and you will still punch with the heaviness.

You can test your snap (and improve it) by lighting a candle and trying to blow it out with the breeze created by your strike.

This heaviness is flowing energy, also referred to as chi, and it can be applied in all movements. The concept of chi is explored more in the Chi Sao chapter.

Adding Movement to the Lead Straight

Standing still and practicing a strike on a stationary or imaginary target is good for developing technique but in a real fight your opponent will not be still, and if you are still you will get hit.

When throwing the lead straight you must constantly protect your head from attack. Vary its position and keep your rear hand up. With everything you do, variety, variety, variety. Keep your opponent guessing.

Using the advance shuffle with a lead straight is extremely useful for closing ground to attack and will also increase power in your strike.

In all hand strikes the hand moves before the foot (in all foot techniques the foot moves first).

Keep your head straight to begin with and move it as necessary depending on the situation.

Initiate the punch then shuffle forward. The hand moves first but the leg movement follows very closely. It is almost at the same time and to the observer it will look simultaneous.

The punch must hit your target before your foot lands on the floor otherwise all the power will go into the ground instead of your strike.

When advancing with any strike it is one coordinated movement.

A strike made while retreating will lose a great deal of power. If you want the blow to be effective you need to quickly stop your backwards movement and shift your weight slightly forward to make the offensive strike before continuing your retreat.

Target Areas

When fighting it is preferable to hit your opponent in the places that will end the fight the fastest.

When considering targets go for those that your opponent leaves open and those that are closest to hit. Use your longest weapon to the nearest vulnerable target.

The two primary targets in fighting are the eyes and the groin. Other preferred target areas are presented in the following diagram.

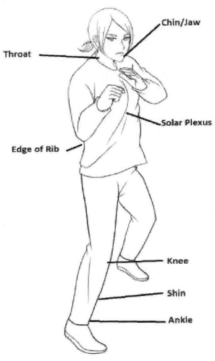

This does not mean that you can/should not aim for other places. There will be many times where these targets may be hard to reach/impractical to aim for.

When training, whether striking a pad, in the air etc., always imagine a target area. When sparring, be accurate about where you are striking.

Slipping

Slipping is an evasive technique used against a straight punch (jab, cross, lead straight, etc.) which allows you to evade a strike, stay in striking range and have both hands free to counter-attack.

Ideally you want your opponent's attack to miss you by as little as possible. Timing and spatial judgement are the key factors.

The basic idea is to turn your shoulder and body to one side so the strike goes over your shoulder. You want to end up near your opponents elbow. This is the perfect time to counter with a strike of your own.

Assuming you are in a right lead OGP and you want to slip the strike over your right shoulder just rotate your right heel counter-clockwise. As you do this shift move your weight to your rear leg, bend your rear knee and turn your shoulder in the same direction as your heel.

Slipping outside the punch (so you are on the outside of your opponent's guard, left picture) is safer but slipping inside (right picture) can be useful also.

To practice slipping stand in the OGP but with your hands behind your back. Have your partner throw straight strikes for you to slip. Start slowly and leave the punch out so you can judge where you are. As confidence/skill builds increase speed and retract the punch.

Parrying

Parrying is a quick hand motion used to deflect blows away from you. It is preferred to blocking which uses force to stop a blow. In parrying, timing and economy of motion are important, not force.

Only parry when needed and at the last possible moment. Also, only move as much as needed to deflect a strike and/or create openings for counters.

Parry's are not your first line of defense (evasiveness and footwork are preferred) but they are used often in a fight.

There are four basic parry movements. For all of them your elbow stays relatively fixed while you use your hand and arm to make the movement.

Most of the time you will parry with your rear hand which leaves your lead free to counter.

When parrying without a counter you can shift your weight slightly over your rear leg. This will increase distance which in turn gives you more time to react. When simultaneously parrying and countering your weight will shift forward.

Inside High Parry

The inside high parry is probably the most used parry since most attacks are punches to the face. It angles the attack away.

Assuming you are in a right lead OGP meet the strike with your rear hand using a slight counter-clockwise twist of your wrist.

The following picture shows the parry as it would be if everything were perfectly symmetrical but in a real fight this will very rarely be the case. It also shows the simultaneous counter of a lead straight.

Clench your fist against a kick or other strong strikes. This can be applied to all parries.

Inside Low Parry

The inside low parry can be used against an attack as low as your groin.

Assuming you are in a right lead OGP your rear hand makes a semicircular, clockwise, downward motion.

When countering at the same time, as your hand parry's shift your weight to your lead leg, bend your knee a little bit and counter with your lead hand.

Outside High Parry

Whereas the inside high parry angles the attack away, an outside high parry is more of a slap. It diverts the attack on the opposite side of your body, i.e., your hand comes across your body.

Outside Low Parry

The outside low parry deflects a blow downward, just like the inside low parry does, but it crosses over your body. It is useful against a mid-level kick.

Against a fast opponent you may need to move back whilst parrying. Do not lean back. Use your footwork. Your rear foot must move before the attack and the parry must be made while your back foot is in motion, not before you begin to move it or after it has landed.

How far you step back depends on your opponent's movements. Ideally, you want to keep the fighting measure so you can counter-attack, however, it is better to go too far back than not enough.

Slip and Parry

Often a high parry is used with a slip. In this case the slip is the main defensive maneuver whilst the parry is more like a back-up. The picture shows slipping outside, but it can also be used slipping inside, and with inside or outside parries.

Always vary your parries, even against the same attacks. To train your reflexes in parrying have a partner throw a mixture of straight attacks. High, low, left and right. Parry as appropriate.

Parry Variations

Although there are only four basic types of parries, like everything in JKD, there are variations. How you apply and/or variate them must be experimented with so you can find what works best for you.

Semi-Circular Parry

The semi-circular parry is used when you have to deflect an attack made on the opposite line that your hand is, either high or low.

For example, if your rear hand is held high as in the standard OGP but your opponent attacks your stomach. For whatever reason you cannot or do not want to use your lead to parry, then your rear hand must come down. It will do a half circle movement to do so.

Circular Parry

The circular parry is not as fast as the basic parry's but it protects a larger area and is more difficult to get past. Just before your opponent's attack reaches its destination you meet it with your hand. Envelop your opponent's wrist to deflect it off its target and then continue to do a full circle so that his/her hand is brought back to its original place, i.e., where you first made contact with it.

If the attack is high then your circular parry will meet your opponent's hand from underneath. If the attack is low then it will meet it from the top.

Counter-Attack

A counter-attack is when you attack your opponent as a response to his/her failed attack, usually due to your defensive act.

When your opponent's attack fails he/she needs time to recover. When you counter you take advantage of this recovery time. You have a greater chance of landing the hit as opposed to if you initiated the first strike.

For every lead there are many possibilities of how to counter. Experiment and select what works best for you in different situations. During training drill (repetitive action) the counters you select so they become instinctive.

You can deflect and then counter as two separate moves (or more if you deflect several strikes), but it is far more effective to counter immediately or even at the same time as your defensive action. A step forward may be needed.

The counter following a parry is called a riposte. The closer in time your riposte is to the parry the better, preferably at the same time or even slightly before the parry.

Assuming you have waited until the last possible moment to parry, then your riposte will occur just as your opponent's attack ends and before he/she can switch to defense. This is known as an attack on completion.

If your opponent has lunged for the attack then you will catch him/her either during the lunge or during his/her recovery. Either way, your opponent can not move his/her feet during this time, which means he/she cannot move away from your strike.

In general, any time the opportunity to counter arises, take it.

A slip and counter is preferred over the parry and counter because it will allow you to hit harder.

After a successful counter you must continue to attack your opponent until he/she is either down or fights back. Do not let him/her rest.

These pictures show a slip and counter, with the parries being a backup to the slip.

This chapter has just covered the basics of countering. The counter-attack is actually a very advanced action and it will be re-visited in later chapters as appropriate.

Side Stepping

The side step allows you to move out of the line of a straight attack whilst staying in range to strike. That does not mean that you have to wait until your opponent attacks before you use it.

If you are using it to avoid a strike then you want to move quickly just before your opponent's strike lands. Only move just enough to avoid the blow. Watch out for your opponent's follow-up.

It doesn't matter whether you are in a right of left lead. Whichever way you are moving, that is the foot that moves first, e.g., if moving right, your right foot moves first.

Against someone with a left lead side step to your right more often, away from his/her rear hand. Against a right lead side step mostly to your left. Sometimes you may go against this rule of thumb to confuse your opponent.

Side Stepping Right

To demonstrate we will assume a right lead stance.

Lean slightly to the right just before you move your right foot about 18 inches to the right and slightly forward at the same time. Shift your weight to the right leg momentarily whilst you move your left foot to re-adopt the OGP. Like all footwork, it is a smooth movement.

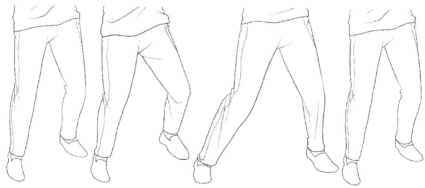

Side Stepping Left

To move from right to left just do the same but move your left foot first

Mirroring Footwork Drill

This simple exercise helps to develop your footwork as well as visual awareness and speed of reaction.

Adopt the fighting measure with your partner. One of you is the leader. The idea is to mirror the leader's footwork, e.g., if your partner is the leader then when he/she moves forward, you move back, or if your partner moves to his/her right, you move to your left so that you stay in front of him/her.

Quick Steps

Quick steps are used to rapidly cover distance, usually of eight or more feet. This is done with several steps.

Quick Advance

With your lead leg take a small step forward, about three inches.

Your rear foot immediately moves to take the original place of your lead. As your rear foot approaches your lead, slide your lead foot forward. This happens in one smooth movement.

For your next step do the same but do not take the initial small step with your lead. The steps are made at a normal walking distance.

The initial short step allows you to move evenly. Without it the rear foot would be doing the majority of the work.

When you finish taking steps adopt the OGP.

Quick Retreat

The quick retreat is the quick advance in reverse except that the initial small step is not done. Begin the quick retreat by moving your lead foot back. As soon as you begin to move your lead foot back start to move your rear so it is out of the way before your lead takes its place.

Sparring

Sparring is as close to fighting as you can get without actually fighting and should be a regular occurrence in your training. It is the best time to practice and experiment with different strategies and techniques, discover your strengths and how to maximize on them, and also to discover your weakness and how to overcome them.

During sparring you should wear protective equipment. The protective equipment is there so you do not get hurt whilst fighting but do not rely on it to protect you. Fight as if you have no protective equipment, otherwise you will become careless with your defense.

Vary your sparring partners so you do not get too used to a certain type of fighter.

Ensure your mouth is closed with your teeth together.

Never look away from your opponent. Learn not to blink during a fight. On the flip-side, if you can cause your opponent to blink or be distracted in some other way then that is a good time to attack.

In order to disguise your intensions keep your eyes fixed on your opponent's eyes. Use your peripheral vision to see his/her whole body. In close fighting watch your opponent's lower line instead of his/her eyes so you can protect your face.

Tapping Out

Tapping out is something you can do when you submit/give up, e.g., when a lock starts to hurt. Tap your training partner at least twice so that he/she feels it. Your partner must disengage immediately. If you cannot reach your opponent then tap the floor. A verbal tap out can also be used, e.g., "stop".

Strategic Fighting Overview

Fighting strategy is covered throughout this book, and some has already been covered, e.g., counter-attack. The aim of this chapter is to give an overview of strategy so you can begin to develop the mindset of a strategic fighter.

It is necessary to have fairly decent technical ability before being able to apply strategy and at least basic reactions must be instilled in your muscle memory to take advantage of openings. You may not be at this stage yet but having tactics in the back of your mind is good practice.

A fight is a flow of movements, and every movement you or your opponent makes has an ongoing effect. Every punch creates an opening, there is a counter for each opening, a parry for each counter etc.

Fighting strategy is all about outsmarting your opponent so that you can hit him/her without getting hit yourself. Many fighters do not care about or do not know fighting strategy. These fighters rely heavily on their mechanical movements (punching, kicking, parrying, countering etc.)

As a Jeet Kune Do practitioner you also rely heavily on mechanical movements but you train them to be instinctive, e.g., automatically striking when an opening arises. When your mechanical movements are instinctive it leaves your mind free to strategize.

When you first come across an opponent study his/her habits, weaknesses and strengths by testing a variety of techniques. Once you have studied your opponent you can structure a plan to exploit his/her weaknesses whilst staying away from his/her strengths. Attack your opponent's weakness and keep him/her on the defensive so he/she cannot rest. Strike from all angles and steadily increase your pace. Don't let up when he/she is in trouble.

As you improve you will be able to anticipate several moves ahead by reading your opponent and/or manipulating his/her actions.

Strategy is basically problem solving, and the problem to solve in fighting is how you can successfully attack your opponent whilst staying protected yourself. The more complicated your solution the more that can go wrong.

Start with the simplest solutions first and escalate as needed until you find what is necessary to solve the problem.

Whatever tactics your opponent favors, do the opposite (kick a boxer, get in close on those that like to use long range techniques, etc.). An exception to this rule is against a defensive opponent. It is unwise to continuously attack one who is careful.

All strikes must have a purpose, either to hit or create a reaction, and you should not strike unless you are certain that purpose will be fulfilled. Missing a strike you are committed to will put you off balance and throwing strikes with no purpose is a waste of energy. When you do strike, do so with full intention and determination. Do not hesitate.

Vary your movements and tactics so you do not become predictable. Change plans of attack when needed, but do not stray too far from your base principles.

Strategy in Distance

When you first come across an opponent and/or do not know his/her intention it is best to keep your distance so you can study him/her.

Once you have a plan you can close in to your preferable fighting measure. Learn your opponent's foot pattern, length of step etc. and adjust to it so you can keep your fighting measure.

If you need to retreat, only do so just far enough to not get hit. That way you can still counter.

Close range (in-fighting) usually occurs when someone moves in to attack. Defense becomes harder, kicking ability is diminished and the probability of ground fighting is increased. Elbows, knees, head-butts, trapping etc. become very useful.

As soon as you become this close to your opponent put your lead foot next to his/hers to immobilize it.

Remember, do the opposite of what your opponent prefers. If your opponent likes to kick, crowd him/her. If he/she wants to grapple, keep your distance.

Short fighters usually prefer to in-fight.

Be wary of a tall fighters reach. Keep your distance and close in when the opportunity arises.

In order for your strikes to land at the right time you need to launch them just before the opponent is at your desired distance.

Bridging the Gap

Bridging the gap is a term used to describe the act of closing distance, which you will need to do when attacking. Many times this can be achieved with basic advancing footwork, but against fighters who are good at keeping their fighting measure you will need to use other tactics.

Here are some suggestions, but by no means the only ways:

> Wait for your opponent to advance for attack and then move in on his/her lunge. A bonus advantage is that the forward momentum in your opponent's attack adds force to your strike.

> Entice your opponent in by taking a series of steps back and gradually shortening them.

> Cut off his/her path of retreat, e.g., back your opponent into a wall.

> Attack a close target first and then advance.

> Use a combination of attacks to cover your footwork.

> A combination of the above.

When against an opponent that prefers a long fighting measure such as one that has a long reach and/or habitually attacks with an advance in footwork, it is best to close distance as opposed to stepping back when he/she attacks. This will deny the long range opponent the space he/she requires for offense.

Single Angulated Attack

A single angulated attack (SAA) is a single strike which uses the most economical route to get to the target. Basically, you see an opening and strike. Economy of motion and non-telegraphing are very important for SAA to be successful.

Timing

This is an introduction to the concept of timing. Specific aspects of timing are integrated into other chapters.

Having good timing in fighting means performing actions at the right moment. The right moment depends on your objective and what movement you are using.

When studying your opponent you must notice and make adjustments for his/her movement time. With this information you can launch your attacks at the times where it will take your opponent longer to react. Some of these times may be:

> When your opponent is preparing to move.

> During your opponent's movement (he/she cannot change direction mid-movement).

> Upon completion of a technique.

> Upon retraction of a strike (e.g., following an opponent's lead back to his/her guard with a lead straight of your own).

> When your opponent is off-balance physically and/or mentally.

> When your opponent is distracted for any reason.

Open and Closed Lines

When a fighter moves a limb it may create an opening in his/her guard. This opening is an open line and is a good target.

On the other hand, where the limb is moving to becomes the closed line. For example, when a fighter blocks an attack, he/she is closing the line.

Time your strikes so they invade the openings as they are being created. In this way, the opponent's limb is moving away from where you are striking. This takes advantage of the time it takes to change direction.

Cadence

Another aspect of timing is the cadence (speed) of movement. If you are able to dictate the cadence with your opponent then you can use it to land strikes. For example, you can set a cadence by using a similar speed for a number of strikes.

Once your opponent is used to the speed throw a faster or slower strike.

Broken Rhythm

When fighting each movement can be counted as a beat, e.g., a strike at full extension equals one beat. Most people will keep a steady rhythm of these beats. When you break this rhythm (using broken rhythm) the interruption will keep your opponent from establishing or keeping a pattern of attack and it will take time for him/her to adjust.

Since each movement is one beat, to break the rhythm you need to attack on the half-beat, i.e., attack halfway through your opponent's movement.

A full strike (extension and return) can be counted as three half beats. Half (0.5), one (1.0) and one-and-a-half (1.5).

- ➢ 0.5 is the strike coming out.
- ➢ 1.0 is the full extension of the strike.
- ➢ 1.5 is the return of the strike to the body.

Attacking on the half beat means that you would strike either on 0.5, before your opponent can fully extend his/her strike, or on 1.5, by following the strike back and hitting your opponent before his/her next attack begins.

Broken rhythm can be used successfully against a faster opponent. Even with just moderate speed you can interrupt your opponent's rhythm and he/she will not be able to adjust in time to defend against your strike.

It is also useful and relatively easy to employ against a swinging opponent.

Against one who unintentionally uses broken rhythm due to irregular attack, keep your distance and wait for other mistakes to be made, such as overreaching.

Mirroring Footwork Drill with Broken Rhythm

Practice breaking rhythm in your footwork while doing the mirroring footwork drill. For example, pick up half a beat by breaking the rhythm going back and then forward. Push shuffle back and then push forward again before your lead foot touches the ground.

When this use of broken rhythm is applied with a strike you are striking on the 0.5 beat, e.g., advance and retreat to encourage your opponent to close in. As your opponent lifts his/her lead foot to advance you lunge forward with your strike.

Alternatively, you can strike on the 1.5 beat, e.g., your opponent strikes. You push shuffle back to avoid the strike and then return an attack while your opponent is retracting his/her initial strike.

Timed Hit

A timed hit is a counter in which you strike your opponent as he/she is at full extension of his/her strike, a 1 beat.

In the picture below the person on the right is uses a timed hit. As the straight punch comes in he slips and counters so that his return strike lands as her strike is at full extension.

Lead Finger Jab

The lead finger jab is your longest range hand attack and the fastest strike you can do, which makes it difficult to defend against. When doing the lead finger jab do not worry about power. It is all about accuracy, speed and timing.

Holding your hand in the correct manner is important for preventing self-harm. Bend your long fingers so they are closer to your shorter ones and tuck in your thumb to make a "spear hand".

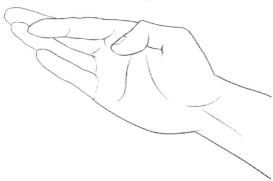

Your hand flicks out to your opponent's eyes. Like all strikes, to get maximum speed you must be relaxed. Do not make any preparatory movements and dart your spear like hand at your opponent's eyes. Your strike lands in front of your nose so that you do not leave any openings in your guard.

Accuracy is very important. If you get your opponent in the eyes it can end the fight very quickly (it is very difficult to fight if you have been temporarily blinded), but if you miss and hit a hard part of your opponent's head or body you may do damage to yourself, especially if you don't form the spear hand properly.

Dropping the Hammer

Described here is the ideal non-telegraphed strike broken down into three concepts. The concepts are not step-by-step. They work together.

The lead straight punch and the lead finger jab strike are the best strikes to use with this.

Perfecting this takes a lot of practice, but it is worth it. When practicing have the defender give feedback as to what he/she saw.

Practicing defense against this will vastly improve the defenders skills.

Constant Movement

Constant movement helps to conceal your strike. If you are still and you begin to move your opponent knows something is happening. If you are in constant movement then there is no "begin to move" because you are already moving.

In your OGP keep your lead arm in a constant weaving motion. When doing this small movement with your lead keep your elbow in basically the same spot, but not rigid.

Track Your Target

Think of your arm as a bow and arrow. It takes time to aim, but once you are aimed all you have to do is release the arrow. When you strike, instead of aiming at the time of striking, already be aimed. Then when you strike all you have to do is release the arrow. In order to already be aimed constantly track your target with your lead hand.

Drop the Hammer

When you use a hammer you should only utilize the part of your arm from your elbow to the hand. It is basically the same movement here. When you strike, drop your forearm on the same level as your target and then just let it fly out.

Snap Back

The snap back is an evasive technique which can be very useful against a straight strike to the head.

As the strike comes in you snap your body just out of distance and then come straight back, usually with a counter.

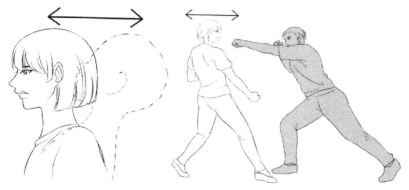

Creating Openings

A skilled fighter that keeps a good guard will rarely just present openings for you to strike. You must create them yourself. This is done with a preparation.

A preparation of attack is any movement that is made with the intent to create an opening for a real attack. It can be done a number of ways including (but not limited to) drawing, false attacks, feints, trapping etc. All of these things will be covered in various lessons of this book, but for now we will start with false attacks and feinting.

Continue to create openings until you can deliver a powerful strike.

As with everything in JKD, it is best to keep the combination of preparation and real attack as simple as possible. Against a smart opponent your preparation may have to be more complicated, but your real attack must remain as simple as needed to be effective.

False Attacks

A false attack is when you launch an attack which is not intended to reach its target. Its intention is to produce a reaction from your opponent which you can then capitalize on.

Normally you would not lunge when your intention is a false attack. A slight movement may all be that is needed to create the response needed.

False attacks are also useful to study your opponent's actions and reactions so you can develop a strategy.

Feints

A feint is a type of false attack. It is where you aim a strike at a certain point for the purpose of distracting your opponent from your real attack. For example, you strike and you opponent reacts (e.g., a parry). His/her reaction creates an opening for you to land your real strike.

To get your opponent to commit to his/her movement your feint needs to be as convincing as a real attack.

Against an unskilled fighter feints may not be necessary. In all other cases, keep your feints as simple as needed to get the job done.

Attempting an attack with more than two feints is risky. If your opponent does not respond to your feints revert back to simple attacks.

An opponent may take advantage if you feint too often and/or repeatedly in the same way. Remember, you must vary your movements and tactics so your opponent cannot read your intentions.

You can do a few simple but real attacks before a feint to increase the chance of success.

How fast you make your feint is dependent on your opponent's reaction. In most cases your real attack will be fast no matter what since you want to capitalize on the opening.

Unless your opponent is particularly slow to react, your real attack must follow your feint very closely so that you can capitalize on the opening the instant it is created.

Stepping forward with a feint will add speed and realism to the attack.

By sparring with different opponent's you can discover common reactions to various feint combinations (the combination being the feint followed by the real attack). You should also test every opponent since different things will work against different people, and may also illicit different responses. By discovering/knowing an opponent's likely reaction you can strike on the anticipation of that reaction.

Combinations of feints must be practiced until they are instinctive and should be tested during sparring. Here are some you can experiment with:

> Bend your lead knee and extend your lead hand a little. Now step in with your lead foot and do a half thrust with your lead arm. As your opponent parry's pull back your hand and then do a real strike. With all feints, only extend your limb as much as needed to induce a response.

> Throw a strike to your opponents head to distract him/her and then quickly attack the shin or knee with a low side kick.

➤ The one-two feint is where you feint and then hit. Where-ever you do the feint, do the real attack on the opposite line, e.g., feint to the head and strike to the stomach, or feint to the left and then strike to the right. The feint must be long to induce the parry, then hit hard and fast before he/she recovers. It is "long-short". Long does not mean slow. It has to do with how deeply you penetrate. The feint must still be fast.

➤ A two-feint attack is "long-short-short". A long feint induces defense and allows you to close distance. Then you do a short feint and then finally the attack, e.g., two feints to the head and strike to the body.

➤ Against a skilled opponent you may need to use "short-long-short". The first feint is short, intended for your opponent to perceive it as a feint and not react. The second feint is long, so your opponent thinks it is the real attack. When he/she reacts to the second feint you deploy your real attack.

➤ The step-in step-out feint is when you step forward with one step showing intention of striking, but then instead of landing the punch you either pivot to the outside with the lead leg or quickly step back before your opponent can counter. You may do this a number of times or just once. Your aim is to make your opponent complacent, and then when the time is right, step in as if to feint but instead deliver a real strike.

Make a series of false attacks and/or feints to get your opponent in the mindset of expecting complex movements and then catch him/her by surprise with a simple attack.

You can use a false attack to provoke an attack from your opponent. You then counter his/her attack. This method of countering is preferable over countering an attack that you haven't induced because you will have a better idea as to what is going to happen.

Use a feint to induce a parry and counter from your opponent. You then parry his/her riposte and deliver a counter of your own. This is known as a counter-riposte.

When defending you want to avoid reacting to false attacks. To hone your perception have your partner throw a mixture of strikes and feints at you. Do your best only to react on the real strikes. The real strikes your opponent throws at you should actually be real. They do not have to be 100% in terms of power but you want it so that if you don't defend sufficiently you will get hit. Use proper equipment, e.g., boxing gloves.

A strategic fighter will be able to determine a pretty good probability of his/her opponent's reactions, but nothing is certain. For this reason you must be able to change your intended movements instantaneously according to your opponent's reactions. Make use of opportunities as they arise. Follow up on each opening and continue to create more until you have finished the fight.

Direct and Indirect Attack

A direct attack is one that begins and ends on the same line. A SAA with no preparations or false attacks is a perfect example, i.e., a single strike.

The direct attack can involve a feint if the feint is on the same line. For example, you throw a strike and then have a slight pause just before impact. This is known as a broken-time attack.

An indirect attack is one that starts on one line but finishes on another. For example, if you feint low and then hit high.

In JKD almost all attack is indirect.

Stop Hit

A stop hit is a prime example of simultaneous offense and defense. It is when you use a strike to stop/intercept an opponent's advance. The advance may be closing distance, an attack, a false attack, etc. Either way, the idea is to use the stop hit to stop the advance as it un-folds, preferably as your opponent begins an attack and/or steps forward. Essentially you are beating your opponent to the attack. You may want/need to use other maneuvers such as parries, false attacks etc. to help facilitate the stop hit.

"When the distance is wide, the attacking opponent requires some sort of preparation. Therefore, attack him on his preparation of attack"

Bruce Lee

The stop hit can be used as a single defensive maneuver, as a counter, with evasive movements etc.

Anticipation and timing are important factors in order for you to be able to hit your target whilst not getting hit yourself.

Lean in or step forward and/or angulate your body to meet the attack if needed.

The most common strikes to use for a stop hit are leading straight ones such as the lead straight punch, lead finger jab, side kick etc.

Suggested times to use a stop hit:

- ➤ When your opponent telegraphs his/her intentions.
- ➤ On your opponent's preparation to step forward.
- ➤ When your opponent uses a wide feint.
- ➤ To stop your opponent's attack while his/her arm is still bent.
- ➤ Against those that come too close.
- ➤ Against those that make wild swings without keeping covered.
- ➤ Against those that habitually feint.

From the time your opponent thinks about making an attack to the time his/her body starts moving takes time. As your perceptive skills improve you will be able to intercept his/her strike at the instant it begins.

False attacks can be used to entice an attack for you to stop hit.

Practice the stop hit often with various appropriate strikes and from different angles.

To practice your timing and distance with stop hits have your partner put on a punching pad. As he comes towards you use a lead straight punch or another appropriate strike to hit the pad. Your aim is to hit the pad at the end of your strike.

Your partner can use many variations which you can adjust to such as distance, speed, height etc.

An opponent whom stays just out of range, has non-telegraphed movements and is well protected in his/her guard position is probably good at interception. Induce a stop hit with long feints if he/she is calm and short ones if he/she is nervous. Follow-up on the feints with trapping or grappling.

Lead Jab

The lead jab is like a less powerful version of the lead straight. It is mainly used early on to study your opponent but can also be used throughout a fight if needed.

During the fight you can use the lead jab can help create openings, as a stop hit, to "stiff arm" your opponent away from you and/or to keep him/her off-balance.

From the OGP your lead hand snaps out into your target and returns without dropping. As it lands the chin is tucked down and protected by your shoulder. Use a vertical fist as opposed to the traditional boxing jab where it is horizontal.

The jab is best aimed at the face since its lack of power will mean hardly any effect on the body. If you cannot get at your opponent's head or body aim for his/her bicep.

Throwing multiple jabs is a good way to keep your opponent busy or to follow up on an initial missed jab.

Low Lead Side Kick

Knowing how to deliver a kick properly gives you a great advantage over a non-kicking opponent. The leg has a greater reach and more power than the arm. Also, kicks are harder to defend against.

Kicks that snap from the knee are best to use as they are faster and more powerful.

Like punches, train to be able to throw kicks from all angles, at all levels of height and whilst moving.

The side kick is both fast and powerful. The low lead side kick to the lead shin or knee uses the side kick, one of your longest weapons, to the closest target. The shin and knee are also hard for your opponent to protect.

The low lead side kick to the knee/shin is useful to keep an opponent at bay or to close the gap so you can attack in combination. A solid side kick to the knee can even be a fight finisher.

Assuming you are in a right lead OGP slide your lead foot forward a few inches. As soon as possible bring your rear foot up just behind your lead. Lift your lead foot and twist your hips as you thrust the edge or flat of your foot into your target. Lean away from your opponent as you kick so you are out of reach. All of this is one smooth motion.

Attacking the rear leg is uncommon in Jeet Kune Do but it may be useful against an opponent who places his/her weight on the rear foot instead of taking a short step back. When your opponent places the all his/her weight on the rear leg he/she will not be able to move away quickly.

Also, if you attack the rear knee while it occupies a lot of weight more damage will be done.

To focus chi into your kicks concentrate on the heaviness of your foot and the energy flowing through your body.

To develop speed do a series of low lead side kicks in the air at an imaginary target. Focus on speed, snap and strength. Keep your eyes focused at your imaginary opponent's eyes as you do it. Looking down will telegraph your intentions.

Stop Kicks

The low lead side kick is very conducive to use as a stop hit, so much so that it is often referred to as the stop kick. It is a useful stop hit against advances, kicks, and since the leg is longer than the arm by attacking the leg you will stop almost any punch before it gets to you.

Besides just using the standard low lead side kick as a stop kick, there are also a few variations, each of which is useful in different circumstances depending on distance, timing etc.

Leg Lift

As your opponent steps in just lift your leg and let him/her run into it. This doesn't have that much stopping power so if your opponent has too much momentum it will not work, but if you have been keeping your fighting measure then he/she should not be able to build that momentum. The advantage of the leg lift is that it is very fast and there is no small slide forward.

Leg Obstruction

This is like a more powerful leg lift. Do the leg lift but torque your body behind it to increase your stopping power.

Experiment with different follow up attacks after the different stop kicks such as the finger jab, lead straight etc. to see what works best for you.

With everything you learn you should be testing what is best for you. When you find those things, favor those movements in training. In this way you are creating your own personalized Jeet Kune Do.

Pendulum Step

The pendulum step is used to quickly retreat and then advance or vise-versa.

When retreating first (from the OGP) quickly draw your lead leg back to just before where your rear leg is. At the very instant that your lead leg is in its new position your rear leg shifts backwards.

At the moment that both feet are together keep both knees bent so you do not waste motion (and therefore time) on any upward motion.

If you want you can stay at this new distance in the OGP. The other option is to reverse the motion so that your rear foot comes up to replace the front foot, and then use your lead leg to counter.

When advancing first you will most likely use the pendulum step with a low level side kick. In this instance the pendulum is used to close range to kick and then recover out of range. It is meant to be very fast.

Intercepting a kick with a stop kick is difficult, especially if your opponent is skilled and/or kicking with his/her lead. In these cases it is better to use evasive footwork to avoid the strike. If the kick is coming from the rear leg, such as a traditional karate type kick, then you have more time to react.

When practicing the pendulum step with a low lead side kick do it against a stationary target to begin with so you can judge distance. Being too close will knock you off balance.

Circling

Circling is a variation of side stepping which allows you to advance at an angle. It is also useful to keep close to your opponent and to help mix up your footwork so you do not become predictable.

Circling Right

Step first with your right foot at an appropriate distance (depending the circumstance) and then pivot around it. Raise you lead hand a little higher than usual in case of a left punch.

Circling Left

Step first with your left foot and then pivot around it.

You can practice circling around any object, preferably something you do not have to look down to see. A punching bag is perfect since you will also be able to throw strikes at it.

A good way to practice all kinds of footwork is to have a partner practice his/her strikes at you while you use nothing but footwork and/or evasive maneuvers (not parries) to avoid getting hit.

Backfist

The backfist is a versatile strike which can be very hard for your opponent to defend against.

Although it is best done from the OGP at shoulder height it can also be thrown from anywhere between your shoulder and waist line. This makes it perfect for attacking from a relaxed non-combative posture if needed.

The primary target when using the backfist is the temple, but other soft parts of the face are also good, e.g., his/her nose.

When striking from the OGP the leading backfist is delivered in an overhand manner using a whip like snapping motion. As you strike your body weight shifts to your lead leg and your rear hand moves down a little bit for protection. It is the top of your largest two knuckles which make contact with your target.

Hook Kick

The hook kick is not as powerful as the side kick and is harder to master, especially if throwing them high, but it is fast and has more versatility.

You have to be closer to your opponent to use the hook kick (in comparison to the side kick) but your recovery time is faster.

The hook kick is best aimed at mid-range vulnerable targets such as the ribs or groin, but if skillful enough it can also make for a devastating head-shot.

From the OGP raise your lead knee so that your thigh is horizontal. Have your rear knee slightly bent and lean back a little. The lower part of your lead leg hangs loose at about a 45° angle. From this position pivot on the ball of your rear foot so that your hips rotate. As you rotate straighten your lead leg. Your rear leg may also straighten. Just before impact snap your foot through your target. All this is one smooth motion with your hip and leg working together.

The hook kick works well with the quick advance. Take the small step forward and slide your rear foot up. Instead of taking the forward step with your lead do a hook kick. You want it to be as smooth a movement as possible.

If you are too close to your opponent you can omit the initial small step forward that your lead takes. Instead just slide the rear foot up and kick.

Front Kick

The front kick is a fast kick which in most cases is aimed at the unprotected groin of an opponent.

Delivery of the front kick is basically the same as the hook kick but is done straight up into the target. Making contact with your instep or shin is preferred, especially if bare-footed.

To increase power in the front kick jerk your hips forward just before you make contact with your target.

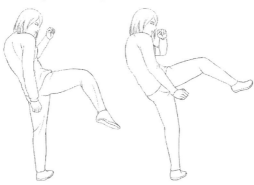

Hitting the bottom of a heavy bag or having a partner hold a punching pad with his/her palm facing the floor are good ways to practice the front kick.

Inside Kick

The inside kick is another fast kick which is useful against an opponent in an un-matched stance, e.g., if you are in a right lead and your opponent is in a left lead. Its main targets are the groin and inside thigh.

The inside kick is delivered similarly to a front kick but on a slight upward slant, opposite to that of a hook kick. Make contact with your instep. Power can be increased with the same hip jerking motion that can be done with the front kick.

Medium Side Kick

This chapter concentrates on doing the side kick at a medium or high level. The lower you aim the easier it is to stay balanced, but often more damage can be done on higher targets. Also, different circumstances will present different opportunities so being able to kick at different levels is useful in fighting.

When aiming higher you must exercise more caution than if kicking the shin or knee because it gives your opponent more opportunities to defend such as blocking, parrying, side stepping, retreating, grabbing your leg etc. Correct timing and delivery (technique, feinting etc.) will ensure your safety. Also, a powerful side kick may just go straight through an opponent's block.

The delivery of the medium or high side kick is basically the same as the low lead side kick except that you aim higher. When doing multiple side kicks just follow the previous one in the normal manner but omit the initial small slide of the lead foot that you did with the first one, i.e., the first kick has the initial slide but every consequent one does not.

To train speed stand with your feet parallel. Alternate side kicks one after the other, i.e., right, left, right, left etc. When you finish one kick put your foot back in its original position. Just before it lands your other foot starts in motion. Alternate kicks as fast as you can.

When kicking the heavy bag, after you have kicked it wait for it to swing back and kick it again.

If you want to hit something solid and don't have anything better just kick a wall. As long as you strike it with a flat foot you won't hurt yourself, you will just get bounced back.

If you have a training partner, after you have kicked the bag the first time have him/her hold it on a slanted angle so you can do a second kick immediately after the first.

Burst

The burst is used to very quickly advance for attack or to retreat. A single burst forward or back should cover the distance of at least two natural steps.

Forward Burst with Side Kick

The forward burst may be used for the sole purpose of closing distance but it is more likely that it is incorporated with some type of attack. One of the more common strikes to use with the forward burst is the side kick. Using the side kick with a burst is probably the most powerful strike you can deliver.

From the OGP take a small step forward as in the quick advance. Sweep your lead hand upward to create momentum and distract your opponent. As your hands sweeps upwards your hips swing forward and your rear foot follows. Before your rear foot lands thrust your body forward as you side kick with your lead leg.

During the movement keep your feet close to the floor. The momentum should be forward as much as possible, as opposed to vertical.

As soon as you land adopt the OGP.

When practicing the forward burst with the side kick just concentrate on your footwork to begin with. Close the distance calmly as opposed to hurling yourself toward your target. When you can do it effectively and stay balanced add in the sweep motion with your lead hand.

When you are ready practice it against a heavy bag. Aim at the center of the bag and concentrate on having your foot land horizontally as you kick through the bag with a snap. If the sound is a dull thud as opposed to a crack then you are pushing more than snapping.

Forward Burst with Back Fist

This exercise shows how you can adapt the forward burst with a punch and is also excellent for finessing your burst movement.

Do the forward burst with the hand sweep, but instead of doing the side kick just place your foot down. Do this continuously concentrating on keeping your balance while moving smoothly. Increase speed when you are ready and substitute the sweeping hand with a backfist.

Backward Burst

The backward burst is used like the quick retreat but is faster and covers more distance in a single movement.

Start the movement by pushing off the ball of your lead foot. Your weight shifts to your rear and your lead moves towards your rear. Just before your lead foot lands, your rear straightens to thrust your body backwards. Ideally you will land on the ball of your lead foot just before your rear lands.

You can practice the forward and backward burst with a partner. One of you tries to kick (lightly) the other using the burst. The other person uses a backward burst to avoid getting hit.

Stop Hit Vs Kicking

As previously stated, a stop kick can be used against a kick but it is very difficult and it is better to use evasive footwork to avoid the strike.

Another option is to use a stop hit. A variation of the burst works well for this, but for it to work you have to have a lot of commitment and really thrust yourself forward. There is no room for hesitation.

Sliding Leverage

Sliding leverage is another method of simultaneous offense and defense. As your opponent's punch comes in you throw a punch from your centerline which intercepts his/hers. Your sliding leverage deflects your opponent's strike while still being on path to meet its target. Total commitment is essential otherwise your opponent's strike might over ride yours.

The following pictures demonstrate sliding leverage against an opponent with an un-matched lead. Notice the person on the right has placed his lead foot on the outside of his opponent's so he is outside her guard.

If you are on the inside of your opponent's guard then you must keep your shoulders square. If you try to lean to the side as if you are outside his/her guard then your opponent will have control of the centerline and you will probably get hit.

Attack by Combination

A combination (also known as a compound attack) is an attack made of two or more offensive movements (punches, kicks, false attacks, knees etc.) thrown in natural and quick succession. In doing so you present your opponent with numerous choices which will then lengthen his/her reaction time, as opposed to a SAA where your opponent only needs to consider the one strike.

Often a combination is made from one or more setups (strikes, false attacks etc.) which create openings for one or more of your strikes to land. Other times you may intend for all of your strikes to land.

Your combination should always finish with a successful hit, regardless of how many landed before the final blow.

The success of your attack by combination (ABC) is dependent on your ability to adapt to your opponent's reactions. If you have studied your opponent you will be better equipped to correctly predict his/her reaction, but anything can happen. Cultivate the ability to change your movements instantaneously.

Combinations are useful against those you are good at parrying, and as always, keep it as simple as you can get away with.

A simple and effective combination that you can do with the strikes that have already been covered is to throw two or three lead straights in a row. Something as simple as repeating an attack can be enough to disrupt your opponent's timing allowing you to connect. It is especially useful against a tired opponent.

Alternatively, it can be used as a feint then hit combination. The first is a false attack and then as your opponent attempts to counter you hit him/her with your second one.

If varying your cadence within a combination it is always best to end with a fast motion.

You can repeat a combination so your opponent expects it and then suddenly change it to catch him/her off guard.

Triples

Combinations comprising of three offensive movements are common. A likely use is to use the first two strikes to lower your opponent's guard so the third can make contact.

When your last blow is aimed in the same spot as the first it is known as a safety triple, e.g., you could use a feint to open up your opponent's low-line and follow it with a body blow, then a head shot and then another body blow.

Levels of Attack

Levels of attack refers to the height at which you attack. It is good practice to vary the levels as it is harder for your opponent to defend.

For example, if you throw three punches to the head you are doing all the strikes on one level. Not much movement is needed by your opponent to defend.

If you low kick first and then strike to the head then you are striking on two levels. The first strike creates an opening for the second. It has a much better chance of success. Likewise, a body punch followed by a high punch is also a two level attack.

A kick to the knee followed by a punch to the face and then another punch to the groin creates a three level attack.

Angles of Attack

All strikes come in at certain angles. For example, a lead straight can come in straight on or from a slight angle. A hook comes in from the side whereas an uppercut comes from below. Other punches, knees, elbows etc. can all come in on a variety of angles.

The angle that the attack comes in on depends on the nature of the strike, but is also dependent on your footwork. Shifting your body slightly to the side means the straight punch will come in on a different angle than if standing straight on with your opponent. The reason for doing this is to gain a superior angle, one where you face your target while your opponent is off angle (as in the previous picture).

Being able to gain a superior angle is good, but you must also be able to hit from any angle as well as be able to change path during execution. This applies to all attack, not just combinations.

Although there are common combinations that many find work well, the exact strikes you use, the order they are in, where they are aimed etc. are dependent on you. Everyone is different. You may find that you are naturally better at certain strikes etc. Experiment and find those which you can make work the best.

When creating combinations switch back and forth from leg to hand and vary the heights and angles of attack.

Practice defending against combinations.

Rear Straight Punch

The rear straight punch is more powerful than a lead straight punch and is best used as a counter or as part of a combination. Although there is a slight difference, it is similar/comparable to the rear cross in boxing.

Assuming you are in a right lead OGP sharply rotate your hips clockwise pivoting on the sole of your left foot. As your body weight shifts forward your lead hand adjusts to protect your face. The punch is thrown straight out in front of your nose and hits your target with a snap in your rear shoulder, preferably into the side of your opponent's jaw.

To maximize the force behind the punch make full use of momentum and drive your body behind the punch. Remember to snap, not push.

One-Two Combination

The one-two combination is a fundamental boxing combination which uses the jab (1) to set the opponent up/get you in range and then a cross (2) as the main landing blow.

Any lead followed by a rear straight can make an effective one-two combination. Throw a quick lead (jab, straight, finger strike) while stepping forward. As your lead retracts back to the body throw a powerful rear straight.

The one-two combination is good to use against long range fighters and/or as a counter after the evasive snap back.

Hook Punch

The hook is a good short range weapon which you can use against an advancing opponent, as a follow-up (e.g., after a lead or feint) or possibly as an initial and/or single strike when the opportunity arises, e.g., if your opponent can not move out of the way.

The power of the hook comes from footwork. Do not pull your hand back. It is unnecessary and telegraphs your intention.

From the right lead OGP have your lead heel raised outward and your rear hand high to protect your face with your rear elbow protecting your ribs.

Keep your lead arm loose and rotate swiftly counter-clockwise as your shift your weight to your rear foot. Allow your arm to be whipped forward following the momentum of your body. Keep your elbow sharply bent so your hook does not swing out widely. Just before contact make your arm a bit rigid from the elbow to the knuckles. There is no bend of the wrist or twist of the fist.

Contact is made with a vertical fist with your knuckles pointing in the direction of your strike. Drive the strike through your target and be ready to follow-up or return to the OGP.

The hook works best with footwork and the lead hook will most likely require you to advance in order to reach your opponent. Due to the horizontal angle of this strike any lateral movement by you (such as a side step) or your opponent into the hook will increase its effectiveness.

The lead hook is also very good in close range fighting because it comes from outside your opponent's field of vision and can go around his/her guard.

This has described the actions for throwing a lead hook because it will be used more often. The method is easily adapted to the rear which may be employed in very close range fighting, especially when you are separating from your opponent.

When throwing the hook to the body bend your front knee so your shoulder is about the same height as your target. To put more power behind it, as you throw the hook duck to the opposite side of the hand that is throwing the hook. The kidney can be a good target for lower level hooks.

Being a much bigger target and less mobile than the head means that body blows have a higher chance of landing than head shots.

To defend against a hook when in-close move into it so it passes around your neck.

Ducking

Ducking, like slipping, allows you to avoid being hit whilst staying in range to counter. It is good to use to evade swings and hooks.

Slipping and the snap back are for straight punches. Ducking is for swings and hooks.

To duck, dip your body forward at the waist so the strike passes over your head. Keep your eyes on your opponent. Timing and body awareness is very important. Ducking too early or on a false attack will leave you vulnerable.

Like most movements, ducking is often combined with other maneuvers such as side stepping, countering, weaving, etc.

It is a rare case that you will duck (or do any other evasive action) without countering.

If you do not have a partner you can swing a punching bag and duck as it comes to you.

Bob and Weave

Bobbing and weaving (also known as the body sway) is another defensive maneuver used to avoid a blow whilst staying in countering range. It allows you to slide under and attack to get close and is good to use against taller opponents. A hook is a good attack to counter with.

Bobbing and weaving can be used separately, i.e., just bob or just weave but they usually go together.

The general idea is to bob forward then weave under the attack. Watch out for your opponent's knee as you do it (use your arm to block).

Weaving

Weaving is a circular movement of the upper body (trunk and head) in and out and from side to side. It is based on and often used with slipping. Relaxation is the key to successful weaving.

Weaving Inside

This assumes you are in a right lead with a matched opponent (an opponent whom is also in a right lead). Your opponent throws a lead punch. Slip to the outside then sink and sway underneath the strike. As you do this use hold your guard high and close and place your right hand on your opponent's left arm to prevent it from hitting you.

Weaving Outside

To weave to the outside just do the opposite. Slip to the inside and weave under to the outside of your opponent's guard. Place your right lead onto his/her left shoulder as you do it.

Bobbing

Bobbing is moving the head vertically. It is done by sinking just underneath curved attacks, e.g., hooks. Even at the bottom of the bob you should be able to counter or slip any straight attacks.

Bobbing straight down leaves you vulnerable, especially if repeated, which is why it is used with the weave.

Renewing the Attack

When your initial attack fails to hit its target (falls short, is parried etc. and you immediately make a new offensive action is it referred to a: renewing the attack. This can be done by continuing on the same line o you may pull your limb back for a new action.

The renewed attack can be a spur of the moment move when your initia attack fails, a spare of the moment move with an intentional failed hi e.g., a feint followed by a lead straight, or completely pre-meditated afte careful study of your opponent. The latter has the most chance of succes: and the first has the least.

Renewing your attack is useful against those who:

> ➢ Step back on your attack.

> ➢ Are put off balance during their defense.

> ➢ Leave openings whilst retreating.

> ➢ Hesitate or are slow to riposte.

> ➢ Pull back their limbs when you strike.

It is best to aim your renewed attack at a close target as you press forward. This will keep your opponent off balance both mentally and physically.

Against fighters who continuously advance and/or use renewed attacks keep your distance, but do not just continuously retreat since that is his/her plan. Advancing at the correct time (study your opponent) wil upset his/her attitude and rhythm.

Lead Straight to the Body

The lead straight is not known for being a power punch but a solid lead to the solar plexus has the potential to be a fight finisher. It can also be used effectively to bring down your opponent's guard and open up other targets.

Another option is to wait for your opponent to lead and then throw a fast body shot when the opening is created.

From the OGP keep your rear guard up and drop your body down as you step forward. Move your chin into your lead shoulder. The majority of your weight is transferred to your lead leg as you thrust your fist through your target.

Rear Straight to the Body

The rear straight to the body is a powerful and extremely useful punch. It is well employed in combination, as a counter, after a feint, to draw down your opponent's guard etc.

It is extremely useful against an opponent in an unmatched stance, i effective against tall fighters and is good to use against those who keep their rear hand high when throwing a lead.

From the OGP sink your body down. As you drop down your lead hand becomes your guard. Pivot on your rear foot and shift your weight to your lead leg as you thrust your rear fist straight through your target.

As you return to the OGP keep your lead shoulder raised for protection against your opponent's counter.

To increase power step slightly to your lead side as you strike.

Now that you have a decent arsenal, practice by throwing multiple power punches on the punching bag. Just throw one after the other alternating sides (left, right, left, right etc.) in quick succession.

Uppercut

The uppercut is used in close range and is very effective against wild "head-down hand-swinging" style charges. It can be done with the lead or rear.

Keep your knees bent before striking. As you throw the punch use an upward scooping motion with your closed palm facing you.

Straighten your legs as you engage your target shifting your weight to whichever leg is opposite of the hand you are using to strike, e.g., if striking with your lead your weight is over your rear leg. As you connect come up on your toes and lean back a little.

Whatever hand you are striking with, use your other hand for protection against counters.

Hooks, rear hand body blows and uppercuts are the main punches used when fighting close.

Rolling

Rolling means to move your body with an in-coming strike in order to render it ineffective. For example, if the strike is coming straight at you move backward (a snap back). If it is a hook then you move to either side depending on what side the hook is coming from.

Shoulder Roll

The shoulder roll allows you to roll away from a punch and then return one straight back.

As the punch comes in you just turn your body so that your shoulder deflects it.

The images demonstrate a shoulder roll drill. Your partner throws a real straight which you shoulder roll.

Then you return the same punch. You keep doing this back and forth.

Shovel Hook

A shovel hook is a type of hook that is angled to be thrown inside your opponent's guard. It is one of the shortest range strikes but has a massive impact when done correctly. It also keeps you better protected than the standard hook.

The shovel hook is good to use against someone who tries to clinch (hug) you.

When throwing a shovel hook off your lead hand first tuck your lead elbow in close to your body. If you are aiming for the body your elbow will be against your hips. If aiming for the head hold it against your lower ribs.

Hold your lead hand so that your palm is facing up at about a 45° angle to the sky. This hand angle will allow your striking knuckles to land correctly on your target.

Assuming you are in a right lead, explosively twist your body to your left to send your fist into the target. This picture is from a left lead.

The shovel hook can also be from your rear in a similar manner.

Vertical Hook

The vertical hook is useful as a defense against an opponent's hook while getting your own hit in at the same time, i.e., simultaneous offense and defense.

As your opponent hooks your punch comes up inside his/her hook.

It then arcs over to make contact with your target. Shift your weight over your lead leg as you do it.

As your strike comes up it deflects his/her stroke out of the way. The harder your opponent punches the more he/she will get hurt.

Immobilization Attack

An immobilization attack (IA), also referred to as a hand immobilization attack (HIA), is when you prevent your opponent from moving a part of his/her body and then attack in the opening that is created. It forces an opening and also keeps you protected from the body part(s) that you immobilize.

The immobilization can be done in a variety of ways such as holding, grabbing, pinning, trapping etc. In this book the term trapping is sometimes used to describe all types of immobilization.

An IA can be instinctive (made possible with trapping drills such as Chi Sao) or planned/set-up, and they can be done singularly or as part of a combination.

A basic IA would be to use one hand to pin your opponents arm down whilst your free arm strikes. Ideally you want to also be out of range of his/her free hand while you strike, or perhaps pin both his/her hands with one of yours.

In this example the arm is immobilized by grabbing it. He then pulls her towards him as he strikes.

In this final example the arm is held and a hook kick is delivered to his groin.

Immobilization is not limited to the hands. Arm to leg, leg to leg, his/her head, hair etc. is all possible.

A bind is when you meet your opponent's hand and then direct it diagonally across his/her body from a high to low line, e.g., from high right to low left.

A croise is when the hand is directed from high to low on the same side, i.e., right high to right low or left high to left low. It is NOT done from low to high.

An envelopment is when the hand is directed in a full circular motion. Contact is not lost and it finishes in the same line. It is basically a circular parry and is good to use against those who like to feint.

Pressure is pressing your opponent's hand.

Chi Sao

Chi sao is an exercise which helps develop the sensitivity needed for instinctive trapping and harnesses flowing energy (chi). It also increases body balance and promotes the looseness of the arms and body.

To demonstrate how to do the basic chi sao exercise the first couple of chapters of **How to Do Chi Sao by Sam Fury** are included in this book.

Available from **SurviveTravel.com/Chi-Sao**.

This is a direct excerpt which demonstrates the Wing Chun version of chi sao. After the excerpt is some additional instruction on how Bruce adapted the position of the feet for Jeet Kune Do.

---Start of Excerpt---

Hand Positions

There are 3 main hand positions used in Chi Sao. They are Tan Sao (Palm up Block/Taun Sao), Bong Sau (Wing Arm Block/Bon Sao) and Fook Sao (Bridge-On Arm Block/Fok Sao/Fuk Sao). Practice each of these hand positions separately as well as switching from one to the other.

Tan Sao
Tan Sao is used to limit the opponent's ability to strike straight in. Drive it forward from the center of your body in a slight upward motion.

Ensure the following;

- ⅄ Your palm is open, fairly flat and facing the sky.

- ⅄ There is approximately a 30 degree bend at the elbow.

- ⅄ The whole arm is very slightly towards your centerline.

Bong Sau

Bong Sau is used to redirect the opponent's attack to a neutral position. It is best used when you are already in contact with the opponents arm.

Ensure the following;

- ⋏ The elbow is pointed straight out and slightly in.

- ⋏ The forearm is angled at a 45 degree downward slope in towards the centerline.

- ⋏ The forearm is also angled 45 degrees forward.

- ⋏ The wrist is in the centerline.

- ⋏ The elbow is higher than the wrist.

- ⋏ The hand/fingers continue in the same direction as the forearm.

- ⋏ The upper arm is in a fairly straight line, pointing to the front.

- ⋏ The angle of the elbow is slightly greater than 90 degrees.

Fook Sao

This defensive position is placed over your opponent's arm. Exact positioning is adjusted to fit the situation and is often described as either high or low.

Ensure the following:

- ⋏ The elbow is about six to eight inches from the body and angles in towards the center of your body.

- ⋏ The forearm angles up with the hand open and the fingers hooked down towards the wrist.

Dan Chi Sao

Single Sticky Hands/Don Chi Sao/Doan Chi

The movements in this drill are not to be applied with intent of striking. They are for teaching the feeling of movement and, to begin with, are to be performed gently.

Contrary to the name, it is the forearms that "stick", not the hands. They stay in touch throughout the entire drill.

P1's right arm is in Tan Sao. P2 adopts Fook Sao with his left arm on top of P1's arm. P2 presses his elbow inwards towards his centerline. Both exert a slight forward pressure.

In one motion, P1 uses the Tan Sao to guide P2's left arm off the centerline then attempts to strike with the same hand. P2 defends by dropping his elbow down and inward.

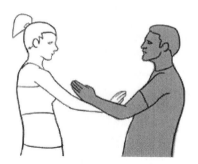

P2 attempts to strike P1's face. P1 defends with Bong Sao. P1 and P2 return to the starting position. They repeat the drill.

Double Dan Chi Sao

This is the same as Dan Chi Sao but with P1's free hand in a Low Fook Sao over P2's Tan Sao. This position does not change whilst the other hand performs Dan Chi Sao as normal. At the completion of one complete round, switch arms. Practice until the switch between arms is seamless.

Luk Sao

Rolling Arms/Lop Sao/Lok Sao

Luk Sao is the base of Chi Sao. Practice it on its own until fluid before incorporating attack and defense drills. Throughout the movement, keep the shoulders relaxed and apply a slight forward pressure.

Note: If your hand positions are correct, forward pressure will automatically be maintained. If your opponent removes opposing pressure, your hand will strike forward by reflex.

Luk Sao is basically moving between 2 positions. From Bong Sao and Low Fook Sao, to High Fook Sao and Tan Sao.

P1's right hand is in Tan Sao. P2's right hand is in Bong Sao. Both of their other arms are in the Fook Sao position situating over their partners opposing arms i.e. right on left, left on right. P1's Fook Sao is in a high position whilst P2's is low. Constantly press the elbow of the Fook Sao into the centerline.

P1 rotates her right elbow up, keeping the wrist in towards her centerline. As her elbow rises up to shoulder height, her forearm drops into the Bong Sao. Her left hand stays in Fook Sao throughout the movement, but moves to a low position. Keep the elbow down on the Fook Sao or forward pressure will be lost.

As P1 one does the above, P2 drops his Bong Sao back down into Ta
Sao. As his Bong Sao drops, he moves his wrist outward and the elbow
lowers back into its drawn-in position of the Tan Sao. As his Bong Sao
settles into a Tan Sao, his Fook Sao moves from low to high while staying
in contact with P1's right Bong Sao.

They then reverse the roll and return to the starting position.

All this is done in a flowing manner and it is important to do it with
intent. Turn and push to interlock the hands. Be tense but flexible.

All drills from now on start from Luk Sao, unless otherwise stated.

When explaining when to initiate a drill sequence from Luk Sao the
terms "high or low point/position" are used. This does not mean the
movement is to be started at the very highest or lowest point. The exact
point of where one should begin a technique is impossible to describe.
With practice you will discover the best timing.

-----End of Excerpt-----

In the above Wing Chun version of chi sao both practitioners stand with
their feet parallel. You can adjust the feet to get an "almost OGP" by
putting one foot forward. This stance will give better balance and
structure.

106

Chi Sao - Lap Sau

This shows how to apply the grabbing technique (lap sau) while doing chi sao.

When your hands are at their closest together use your rear hand to grab your opponent's arm.

Pull your opponent's arm over his/her other arm and pin it down as you backfist with your lead.

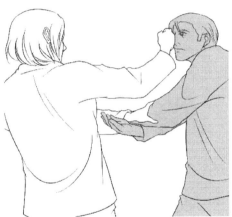

Your pulling action also pulls your opponent into your strike for added power.

In a real fight you will not be doing chi sao. Here is one of the many ways in which the lap sau can be adapted to a more realistic situation.

As your opponent advances with a lead straight use a stop kick in conjunction with a parry. Your parry turns into a lap sau grab. Pull your opponent in as you fire a lead straight of your own.

Chi Sao – Phon Sau

This shows how to apply the trapping technique (phon sau) while doing chi sao.

During chi sao, when you feel your partner's energy being disrupted initiate phon sau. At the right moment, disengage chi sao and bring one of your hands over both of your partner's hands. Pin his/her hands down and use your other hand to strike.

Elbows and Knees

Elbows and knees are fast and powerful fight finishers. This is because they are harder and less fragile than the bones in the hand and they can be delivered with much greater force behind them.

Elbows

From the OGP sharply twist your hip and pivot on the ball of your foot (the same side of the elbow you are striking with). Snap and drive your elbow into your opponent's face, preferably his/her jaw.

Your hand is kept open to expose the bone. Keep your elbow close to your body and your arm loose until the last moment. Your wrist stays limp.

As in all strikes, power comes up from the ground and from the pivot in your hips.

Elbows can come in from a variety of angles.

For added power, grab your opponent and drive his/her head into your elbow as your strike.

Knees

Knees can make contact from a variety of angles.

Pull your opponents hair/head/ears down and drive your knee into his/her face. Point your foot and toes down for protection.

Extend your hips and come up on your toes to increase force. Do a few consecutively for more damage.

A knee to the groin is also very effective. If needed, hold your opponent's shoulders.

Pressing

Pressing your opponent is a good way to keep him/her off-balance. It is done by crowding your opponent so he/she can't attack. You can attack when gaps are created. This even works well if you are out-weighed.

Pressing is basically continuously shoving into your opponent using your hips and shoulder to apply force. Your weight shifts to your lead foot and you use the advance shuffle to press into him/her. Use your hands and body to trap your opponent and then strike when the opportunity arises.

Self Defense Scenarios/Instinctive Training

Often martial arts have specific ways to handle certain situations which the students drill. This can be a great way to train muscle memory so if that particular situation arises the movements are automatic. The problem is that these movements often rely on specific conditions on the situation, but in reality there are many variables. Also, everybody is different. What may work for you may not work for me.

With instinctive training you train to react quickly to all types of situations, as opposed to reacting a particular way for a particular situation.

Often the better way to handle any surprise attack/self-defense type scenario is to use a simple strike to a primary target such as a finger strike to the eyes or a kick to the groin (as opposed to complicated escape maneuvers, joint locks etc.). This initial strike will create time and distance so you can continue to fight as normal, or it may be all that is needed to end the encounter.

Use of Force

Fighting off an attacker that is trying to do serious harm to you is different than a sparring session or a scuffle with your friend. Different situations call for different degrees of force. It is up to you to decide.

In a potentially life-threatening situation, anything goes. Don't forget about head-butts, back heels, hair pulling, biting etc.

Do what you need to do to escape, but know that your actions have consequences. If you are too excessive you may get in trouble with the law.

Awareness

By being constantly aware of your surroundings you can avoid being surprised. This can be challenging for those that are used to "living inside their heads", but if you constantly remind yourself to notice your surroundings it will soon become second nature.

Having a wide peripheral vision will increase your ability to perceive what is happening around you. To improve you peripheral vision focus on a landmark in the distance, e.g., a tall building. Keep looking at the landmark but instead of focusing on one point open your field of vision and notice as much as you can in the corners of your eyes.

Attitude

When you are able to stay relaxed in tense situations you will make better choices and also be able to react faster. Panicking is never good.

Notice the times when you are relaxed. Practice reproducing this relaxed feeling throughout your day, especially when you are feeling stressed.

Being able to relax is good but only constant practice will develop confidence in your abilities. This is especially true if against armed and/or multiple assailants. The last thing you want to do is freeze up.

Palm Heel

A palm heel is a good striking weapon in self-defense, especially to the head where there are a lot of hard bones that may damage your knuckles. It can replace the fist in most cases with little or no other variations needed.

Make sure it is the heel of your palm that makes contact.

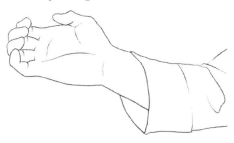

Instinctive Training Scenarios

Have a training partner attack you at random. React with the object of taking him/her out as quickly as possible.

Here is a list of random situations that you can react against, and any others you think of. Where applicable, practice these things from all angles and variations, e.g., front, side, back, from different positions (on the ground, sitting etc.). Some suggested variations are shown in brackets.

Some general advice has been given. This is taken from **How to Stree Fight by Sam Fury** which also has more specific maneuvers for differer situations.

Available from **SurviveTravel.com/Street-Fighting**.

Common Scenarios

➢ Arm grabs (single, double)

➢ Arm locks (many variations)

➢ Bear hugs (arms free, arms pinned, lifted)

A basic defense against someone grabbing you from behind is to loosei his/her grip enough to face him, attack aggressively, and then escap when you can.

➢ Belt hold

➢ Chest grab (with a punch)

➢ Choke holds

When being choked protecting your airway is paramount. Grab you opponent's arm with both of your hands and jerk down as hard as you can. Tuck your chin down in the gap you create and towards his/he elbow. From here, work to loosen his/her grip and attack any way you can e.g. bite, bend fingers, kicks, attack groin etc. Tucking your chin i good choke preventative.

➢ Half/Full nelson

➢ Head locks

➢ Stomped on the ground

➢ Tackles

➢ Wrist grabs (single, double)

➢ Wrist locks (many variations)

Multiple Assailants

➢ Approached from multiple angles

➢ Being held in various ways and attacked

When facing multiple opponents the threat rises exponentially. Stay on your feet and use your surroundings to create a situation where you are only facing one opponent at a time, including putting them in each other's way.

Armed Assailant

- Swings/slashes, thrusts
- Club
- Knife
- Staff

When faced with an armed opponent do your best to keep your distance. Try to place stationary objects between yourself and your attacker. When your opponent strikes move out of the line of attack and/or redirect the weapon away from you. Secure the weapon and/or the limb holding the weapon. Attack hard and disarm him e.g. bite, arm lock etc.

Defense Against Guns

The action you decide to take when faced with a gun, e.g., compliance, running away, disarming etc. will depend on you and the situation. Usually it is best to comply, especially if the demands are purely materialistic.

It is difficult to aim accurately with a hand gun if the target is more than 10 meters away, especially if the target is moving erratically. If the assailant has a shotgun or rifle then his/her ability to accurately shoot increases.

If you decide to run be erratic in movement e.g. roll, zigzag etc.

If you are within arm's reach, grab hold of the gun whilst staying out of the line of fire. Twist it away from you and towards your assailant.

Progressive Indirect Attack

A progressive indirect attack (PIA) is an attack in which you create an opening and land your real strike without withdrawing your limb.

When you strike in a single, forward movement without any feint or other false attack it is a SAA.

When you feint and then strike in two movements, such as moving your limb back or using a different limb to make the strike, you are using ABC (in this example case the combination is a feint followed by a single angulated attack).

In PIA you feint to create the opening and then you shift lines to strike the opening.

In PIA the object of the feint is to entice a response and to close distance hence the word progressive (you progress toward your target). It conceals your lunge forward. This lunge should cover at least half the distance between you and your opponent.

The attack is indirect because you change lines, as opposed to a SAA (also known as Single Direct Attack) which goes directly onto the target.

When you feint your opponent moves to defend. As his/her defensive move (block, parry etc.) is moving towards your feint you change the line for your real attack, e.g., with a small circular motion. This is known as a dis-engagement because you are dis-engaging from the line of attack (when your limb meets your opponent's limb it is an engagement). Your dis-engagement should pass very closely to your opponent's hand but it must stay ahead of the defensive action. Except in rare cases, make this movement as small as possible.

Your second movement (your real attack) usually only happens in the second half of the distance. Your feint is in the first and it must be long enough to allow your opponent to act upon it.

An example of PIA is to throw a low lead feint to the groin. When your opponent drops his/her guard you straighten your legs and strike his/her head.

Against someone who habitually disengages, feint your preparation and then use an immobilization attack.

Attack by Drawing

Attack by drawing (ABD) is when you entice your opponent to make an attack which you can then intercept or counter against.

The opening may be made one of three ways:

1. By exposing a target, e.g., drop your guard and when your opponent attacks your head strike him/her low.

2. By performing a false attack or other action that invites a counter, e.g., feint an attack that your opponent parries and ripostes. You then counter on the riposte.

3. By closing in on your opponent to "force" an attack, e.g., advance into your opponent's striking range and when he/she strikes use a stop hit.

Drawing an attack is preferred to waiting for your opponent to lead on his/her own accord because it gives you a better idea of what your opponent plans to do, i.e., you will already know how you will counter his/her probable reaction to your draw.

When you counter an opponent's counter, such as in the example of the second way to make an opening, it is called counter-time. Counter-time can also be applied to a stop hit. You draw the stop hit with the intention of deflecting it and then countering.

Beat

When you are against a fast opponent that does not fall for feints you can use the beat.

A beat (not to be confused with the half-beat in broken rhythm) is when you hit your opponent's hand (or as close to it as possible) with your hand. Some examples of how the beat can be used are:

> To force an opening, i.e., knocking his/her hand to the side. Make your movement sharp and fast. An immobilization attack makes a good follow up as does renewing the attack or other attacks by combination.

> As the feint part of an indirect attack. Make your movement light and fast so you can quickly pass his/her hand.

> To draw an attack. Make your movement light and not so quick. Often your opponent will beat back, or perhaps he/she will try to attack on the half beat.

Spin Kick

The spin kick can be useful against an opponent who rushes you but it requires you to momentarily put your back to your opponent, which also means you will take your eyes off your target.

It is best used as a surprise counter against aggressive fighters that attack in a straight line without lunging at you. It is dangerous to employ against defensive opponents since they are more likely to be able to take advantage when your back is turned.

The spin kick is harder to master than other kicks but it may be the only kick in which you can catch a skilled fighter off-guard with.

Assuming you are in a right lead OGP stand about a legs length away from your target and adjust your lead foot to begin the spin.

Pivot on the ball of your right foot and then swiftly rotate your body. Keep your eyes on your opponent as long as possible and picture the spot you are aiming for in your mind as you spin.

As you complete the spin thrust your foot straight through the target using the same whip of the hips and snap of the foot on contact. Hit the front of your target in the same manner that a side kick does.

The hand sweep as described in the burst lesson (under the heading Forward Burst with Side Kick) can be used to distract your opponent so you can land the spin kick.

The best way to practice the spin kick is in the air and then on the heavy bag.

Sweep Kick

The sweep kick is rarely used because it is a high kick that can be caught by an experienced fighter. Also, it is not very powerful and you have to be fairly flexible to do it. These things combined make the reward not worth the risk in most cases, however, it is useful against someone who leaves his/her lead foot high while attacking.

This kick is initiated with the quick advance in the same way a hook kick is. Assuming you are in a right lead, when you do the kick your foot travels vertically upwards and then with a small arc from left to right at the top of the motion. Connect with your target using the heel and outside edge of your foot.

Grappling

At the time of his death Bruce Lee was still looking into grappling. Sinc
it was still relatively new to him he did not leave many notes behind bu
he did consider it to be an important area of study.

As a bonus, included now is free access to the complete version o
Ground Fighting Techniques to Destroy Your Opponent by Sam Fury

Bonus – The Complete Version of Ground Fighting Techniques to Destroy Your Enemy

To get your free electronic copy of Ground Fighting Techniques t
Destroy Your Enemy please visit:

SurviveTravel.com/JKD-Bonus-Ground-Fighting-Free.

Claim Your Free Books

Dear Reader,

Thank you for reading **Bruce Lee's Jeet Kune Do**.

I truly hope you got some value from it ☺.

In life I am a big believer in constant improvement, and this is no different in the books that I write.

Receiving (and then acting upon) feedback from readers is (in my opinion) the most effective way for me to improve the books.

Another thing is the effect of positive or negative reviews. The number of reviews and the number of stars left in those reviews can make or break a books success.

In light of these two things I have a favor to ask of you:

It would be greatly appreciated if you would leave an honest, positive review on Amazon

SurviveTravel.com/Jeet-Kune-Do-Reviews

and/or Goodreads

SurviveTravel.com/Jeet-Kune-Do-Goodreads.

Or, if you have feedback that is not so favorable (constructive criticism) then please share it with me directly (as opposed to giving a bad review) and I will address the issues in future editions.

I can be contacted via email: admin@survivetravel.com.

Want more Survive Travel Publications but can't afford them? Discover three ways to **get them all FREE at**

SurviveTravel.com/Three-Ways-Get-Free-Books

Thanks again for your support.

Sam Fury, Author.

About the Survival Fitness Plan

The Survival Fitness Plan is ongoing fitness and mental training in escape, evasion and survival.

It can be broken down into three parts:

1. Daily fitness training.

2. Escape, evasion and survival.

3. Further learning.

1. Daily Fitness Training

When in immediate danger you basically have two options – fight or flight.

Survival Fitness uses fight or flight activities as regular physical fitness training including Climbing, Parkour, Riding, Running, Self Defense, and Swimming.

If you are going to spend time exercising, then you may as well train your body in activities that may save your life at the same time.

2. Escape, Evasion and Survival

Training in all things to do with escaping capture, evading the enemy, and surviving in urban and wilderness environments.

Specific subjects covered include entry and exit techniques, evasive driving, hostile negotiation tactics, lock-picking, urban survival, wilderness survival, wilderness medicine, and many more.

3. Further Learning / Publications

All the basic information you need to train in Survival Fitness is **FREE** to access on the **SurvivalFitnessPlan.com** website.

For those that want a deeper understanding in any particular field there are the Survival Fitness Plan Training Manuals and other related publications. The Survival Fitness Plan (**SurvivalFitnessPlan.com**) is a Survive Travel initiative (**SurviveTravel.com**).

About the Self Defense Series

Self Defense plays a big part in the Survival Fitness Plan daily training and the self defense system created by Sam Fury is relatively easy to learn (it is a minimalist system) and highly effective.

The **Self Defense Series** has volumes on some of the martial arts that were used as a base in the creation of Survival Fitness Self Defense, as well as the final Survival Fitness Self Defense Training Manual.

Volume One: How to Street Fight

How to Street Fight: *Close Combat Street Fighting and Self Defense Training* is a simple, unrefined and aggressive close combat street fighting / self-defense training system and strategic guide.

Includes lessons on:

- Staying safe and minimizing injuries whilst training.
- Achieving the most power from your strikes.
- The best places to aim for without needing pin point accuracy.
- A simple and natural all-purpose fighting stance.
- A variety of training methods.
- How ANYTHING can be used as a weapon, and the best way to use it, no matter what it is.
- The best ways to finish your opponents FAST.
- Striking methods that can be used instantly and are incredibly effective.

... and much, much more.

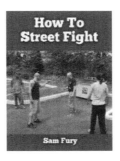

Volume Two: How to Win a Street Fight

This one of a kind street fighting/self-defense training manual and strategic system will teach you the fighting techniques you need to know to inflict maximum damage with minimal effort.

How to Win a Street Fight: *Stand Up Fighting Techniques to Destroy Your Enemy* combines powerful techniques and a straight forward street fighting strategic guide that will shatter your enemies!

Note: How to Street Fight by Sam Fury contains all the information in How to Win a Street Fight plus a whole lot more!

Volume Three: Ground Fighting Techniques to Destroy Your Enemy

Even if you have **ZERO** experience **Ground Fighting Techniques to Destroy Your Enemy:** *Mixed Martial Arts, Brazilian Jiu Jitsu and Street Fighting Grappling Techniques and Strategy* will teach you the best ground fighting techniques and demonstrate how to use them in a systematic method so you can use them effectively whether it be Mixed Martial Arts, Brazilian Jiu Jitsu, Street Fighting or any other ground fighting you come across.

Note: How to Street Fight by Sam Fury contains all the information in this book plus a whole lot more!

Volume Four: Basic Wing Chun Training

Basic Wing Chun Training: *Wing Chun Kung Fu Training for Street Fighting and Self Defense* is a Wing Chun Kung Fu training manual designed to progressively teach basic Wing Chun techniques and principles and shows how to adapt the Wing Chun techniques learnt for use in street fighting and self-defense.

Volume Five: How to Do Chi Sao

Chi Sao (Sticky Hands) is a Wing Chun Kung Fu training exercise used to develop touch sensitivity (as well as having many other benefits).

How to do Chi Sao: *Wing Chun Sticky Hands* will teach you how to enhance your Wing Chun Kung Fu ability in the same way Bruce Lee did and learn to read your opponents' intentions and respond to his movements much faster than you could by eye alone.

Volume Six: Bruce Lee's Jeet Kune Do

Bruce Lee's Jeet Kune Do: *Jeet Kune Do Techniques and Fighting Strategy* is more than a bunch of martial arts techniques. It is a fully useable Jeet Kune Do training manual covering all aspects of Bruce Lee's fighting method in a progressive format.

Upcoming Titles

The following titles are in the process of being written. The actual name of the publication may be different upon release.

Sunbye Self-Defense

In this unarmed self-defense focused volume Sam Fury puts lessons learnt while training in the Philippines onto paper. A unique system created by Peter Sunbye combines a number of martial arts including Lawrence Lee's Tong Kune Do Kung Fu, Wing Chun, Balintawak Arnis Escrima & Panatukan to create a highly effective and relatively easy to learn self-defense system.

Practical Filipino Martial Arts

Kali/Arnis/Escrima are weaponry based Filipino martial arts. This book combines methods learnt from a variety of Arnis/Escrima/Kali grandmasters and focuses on highly practical stick-fighting and knife-defense techniques and training methods. This is the weaponry portion of Peter Sunbye's Self-Defense method.

Sunbye Self Defense Bundle

This volume combines Practical Unarmed Self-Defense and Practical Filipino Martial Arts into one volume so that those who wish to have all the information can do so at a considerable discount, as opposed to buying each volume separately.

Visit **Martial-Arts-Holiday-Philippines.Blogspot.com** to learn more about Peter's Self-Defense system.

Street Self-Defense

One of two official Survival Fitness Plan Self-Defense training manuals.

After decades of training and research Sam Fury puts his highly practical and easy to learn self-defense system into a training manual.

This particular training manual focuses on everything to do with unarmed self-defense including stand-up, ground-fighting and self-defense against unarmed and armed assailants.

Street Self-Defense Weaponry

The second official Survival Fitness Plan Self-Defense training manual with a focus on weaponry.

Street Self-Defense Bundle

The proposed final book in this series is both the official Survival Fitnes Plan Self-Defense training manuals in one big volume so that those wh wish to have all the information can do so at a considerable discount, a opposed to buying each volume separately.

Other Survive Travel Publication Series

Escape, Evasion and Survival

Sam Fury's **Escape, Evasion and Survival Series** covers all things to do with escaping capture, evading the enemy, and surviving in urban and wilderness environments.

Specific subjects covered include entry and exit techniques, evasive driving, hostile negotiation tactics, lock-picking, urban survival, wilderness survival, wilderness medicine, and many more.

Survival Fitness

The **Survival Fitness Series** created by Sam Fury contains all the publications covering Survival Fitness Plan Daily Fitness Training Additional Activities such as swimming, parkour, rock-climbing, etc.

Yoga

Yoga is mainly used in Survival Fitness as a cool down/stretch routine after daily fitness training, but is also recommended as an additional exercise.

Aventura's **Yoga Series** contains volumes with yoga routines specializing in achieving specific goals, e.g., increasing flexibility, therapy, weight loss, etc.

Intimacy

Using her knowledge of massage, tantric practices, and yoga, Aventuras brings to you the adult's only **Intimacy Series** to help you increase and/or rekindle passion in your relationships.

Miscellaneous

The **remainder of Survive Travel Publications** that do not belong to any specific series.

Index

Author Bio

Sam has had an interest in self-preservation and survival (wilderness medicine, self-defense, fitness, escape and evasion, urban and wilderness survival, etc.) for as long as he can remember.

His accumulated knowledge is a result of years of formal and informal training, career related experience and general interest in survival, martial arts, the military, adventure travel and other various outdoor pursuits.

Describing himself as a "Survivalist, Minimalist, Traveler", Sam spends his time traveling the world taking training courses (Jeet Kune Do and Wing Chun in China, Escrima/Kali in the Philippines, wilderness medicine in the US, parkour in Singapore, survival courses in Africa and Australia, etc.) and sharing what he learns through his books.

Follow Sam Fury

SurviveTravel.com/SamFury

Facebook.com/AuthorSumFury

Sam Fury works in close collaboration with SurviveTravel.com and SurvivalFitnessPlan.com.

Facebook.com/SurviveTravel

Facebook.com/SurvivalFitnessPlan

Printed in Great Britain
by Amazon